GERMAN RULE AND SOCIO-ECONOMIC PATTERNS IN TANZANIA

GERMAN RULE AND SOCIO-ECONOMIC PATTERNS IN TANZANIA

Edited by

Sakina Faru

Charles Sanaane

Claus Melter

GALDA VERLAG 2024

Bibliografische Information der Deutschen Nationalbibliothek
Die Deutsche Nationalbibliothek verzeichnet diese Publikation in der Deutschen Nationalbibliografie; detaillierte bibliografische Daten sind im Internet über https://dnb.de abrufbar.

© 2024 Galda Verlag, Glienicke
Neither this book nor any part may be reproduced or transmitted in any form or by any means electronic or mechanical, including photocopying, micro-filming, and recording, or by any information storage or retrieval system, without prior permission in writing from the publisher. Direct all inquiries to:
Galda Verlag, Franz-Schubert-Str. 61, 16548 Glienicke, Germany

ISBN 978-3-96203-400-9 (Print)
ISBN 978-3-96203-401-6 (E-Book)

TABLE OF CONTENT

Introduction
Sakina Faru, Charles Sanaane, Claus Melter i

CHAPTER ONE: In memory of genocide against members of Majimaji Movement in Tanzania from 1905 to 1907
Dr. Sakina Faru 1

1.1 The Setting 3
    1.1.0 Definitions of terms and concepts 3
    1.1.1 Majimaji 4
    1.1.2 Genocide 5
    1.1.3 Afrocentricity 6
    1.1.4 Renaming of Majimaji in Tanzanian context 10
1.2 Discussion 10
    1.2.0 Causes of Majimaji war 11
    1.2.1 Forced cotton cultivation and rubber extraction 12
    1.2.2 Heavy taxation 13
    1.2.3 Compulsory labour and harassment in road construction 14
    1.2.4 Wildlife ordinances 15
1.3 Areas covered by Majimaji war 15
    1.3.0 Consequences of Majimaji war 16
    1.3.1 Devastation and depopulation 17
    1.3.2 Internal changes 18
    1.3.3 Changes from extractive to developmental colonialism 18
    1.3.4 Development and neglect 19
1.4 Majimaji war genocide or not genocide? 19
1.5 Memory pertaining to Majimaji war 24
1.6 Repatriation and reparation 26
1.7 Women and heroines in the Majimaji war 27
1.8 Majimaji heritage Resources 29
    1.8.1 Majimaji heritage sites 29
    1.8.2 Majimaji heritage landscapes 30

1.9 Concluding Remarks 32
References 36

CHAPTER TWO: Cultural Diversity in Tanzania and Germany
By Dr. Sakina Faru 41
2.0 Introduction 41
2.1 Definition of key terms and concepts 41
2.2 Interactions before colonialism 42
2.3 Interactions during colonialism 51
2.4 Interactions during post-independence of Tanzania, to date ... 55
    2.4.1 Religious undertakings 55
    2.4.2 Language interactions (Kiswahili language) 55
    2.4.3 Social services delivery 56
    2.4.4 Training and Exchange of Expertise 56
    2.4.5 Research and Development 57
    2.4.6 Democracy, Gender Equality and Human Rights 57
    2.4.7 Economic and Infrastructure Development 58
    2.4.8 Diplomatic Relations 59
2.5 Concluding Remarks 60
References 61

CHAPTER THREE: Heroines of Majimaji War in Tanzania from 1905 to 1907
Dr. Sakina Faru 65
3.1 Introduction and General Background 65
    3.1.1 Introduction 65
    3.1.2 General Background 65
3.2 Women's Participation in Liberation Struggles 69
    3.2.1 Women's Participation in Wars in Africa 69
    3.2.2 Women's Participation in Majimaji War 72
3.3 Discussions 76
    3.3.1 Perception of wartime statuses in gender relations 76
    3.3.2 Women's Participation in Majimaji War:
           The Unsung Majimaji war heroines 76

3.4 Concluding Remarks 78
References 79

Chapter Four: German built heritage for continued use for socio-economic development in Tanzania
Dr. Charles Bernard Saanane 83

4.0 Introduction 83
4.1 Drivers of exploration and scientific expeditions around the world 83
4.2 Collected Human Remains, Animal Remains, Plant Remains
       and Cultural Objects from Tanzania during German Rule 86
    4.2.1 Collected Human Remains from Tanzania during German Rule 86
    4.2.2 Collected Animal Remains from Tanzania during German Rule ... 90
    4.2.3 Collected Plant Remains from Tanzania during German Rule 91
    4.2.4 Collected Cultural Objects from Tanzania during German Rule 91
4.3 Discussion: Repatriation Endeavours for Remains Collected
       from Tanzania during German Rule 91
    4.3.1 Repatriated human remains from Germany (representing
              extant humans and extinct proto-humans) 91
    4.3.2 Un-repatriated human remains 92
    4.3.3 Background to the stance on repatriation and
              Looming Questions 93
    4.3.4 Looming Questions 95
4.4 Future Prospects 96
References 97
    APPENDICES 100

Chapter Five: German built heritage for continued use for socio-economic development in Tanzania
Dr. Charles Bernard Saanane 105

5.0 Introduction 105
5.1 Infrastructure for Socio-Economic Services 107
    5.1.1 Houses for Governance and Settlements 107
    5.1.2 Electricity Services 109
5.2 Economic Ventures 110

    5.2.1 Establishment of Ports, Warehouses and Customs Services 110
    5.2.2 Establishment of Plantations 110
    5.2.3 Mining 111
    5.2.4 Wildlife Conservation Measures 111
5.3 Establishment and Development of Transport Infrastructure 113
    5.3.1 Railways Construction, Post and Telegraph Stations 113
    5.3.2 Road construction 114
5.4 Establishment of Social Services 114
    5.4.1 Establishment of Schools 114
    5.4.2 Establishment of Healthcare Facilities 115
5.5 Kiswahili Language 115
5.6 Research and Development 117
5.7 Discussion 118
5.8 Future Prospects: Current Collaborations 122
    5.8.1 General Overview 122
References 123

Chapter Six: Responsibility in Germany in relation to the genocide of members of the Majimaji movement and civil society in 1905-1907 in present-day Tanzania

Prof. Dr. Claus Melter 127

6.1 Introduction 127
6.2 It was a genocide 129
6.3 Refusal to recognise the fact of crimes and genocides committed 131
6.4 The power of dethematisation 131
6.5 Remembering the victims of National Socialism 133
6.6 Different memory practices 134
6.7 Concealment of genocides in writings on missions
    and colonial medicine 134
6.8 Colonial medicine and genocide 136
6.9 Learning history 136
Sources and literature 137

The Editors and Authors 145

INTRODUCTION
Sakina Faru, Charles Sanaane, Claus Melter

We, Sakina Faru and Charles Sanaane as researchers from Tanzania and Claus Melter as researcher from Germany, present you texts about the Tanzanian-German History and Herstory. This book deals with the facts of the Majimaji-War, about Gender and Cultural Diversity in Tanzania and Germany, about the Heroines of the Majimaji-War 1905-1907 in Tanzania. The book treats stolen human remains, animal remains, plant remains and cultural materials. It is about German built heritage for continued use for socio-economic development in Tanzania. And there is the responsibility of Lecturers, Researchers and Students with German decent to intensely deal with the Genocide.

Chapter One, "In memory of genocide against members of Majimaji Movement in Tanzania from 1905 to 1907," presents to the point a review of other intellectuals' works in an assortment of disciplines that include History, Literature, Historical Archaeology and Ethnoarchaeology. Such works embrace historical data sets, mainly from unpublished historical sources (outstandingly, archival materials, oral accounts and published data sets). As a matter of fact, the presentation delves into diverse facets to remember, discuss, functionalise or to deny and minimise genocide against members of the Majimaji Movement.

Importantly, the substance of this work owes to the reason that there are many interpretations about Majimaji war based on a fair amount of research ventures but the facts give the impression that leads to many controversial questions. It is evident, for instance, in naming the said movement. The revolts were called in the beginning by German colonists as Majimaji rebellion, while during struggles for independence and after independence in Tanganyika (now mainland Tanzania), the combat was called and is still called, Majimaji war. Accordingly, atrocities and consequences of the war are variously interpreted with some calling genocide to both Africans and Germans, whereas others refrain from declaring the said inhuman undertakings as genocide. The said position owes to current descriptions including some of the primary sources that give chance for questioning their correctness and relevance.

In putting into the right perspective, the chapter sets in by presenting concise definitions of key terms and concepts. They help to show the manner, for instance, naming of the war by various authors and then in this chapter, the suggestion is naming in a single Kiswahili word, Majimaji. Moreover, the term genocide is provided so as to orient readers on its genesis and eventual adoption, in Paris, France on 9th December, 1948, of the United Nations 1948 Convention on the Prevention and Punishment of the Crime of Genocide. The Convention was adopted in recognition of genocidal action as a crime under international law. Besides, the definition of Afrocentricity helps to show an unbiased presentation of the materials in the chapter in declaring that Majimaji war embraced genocide. The reason is that the paradigm does not point any accusing finger by not supporting any racist doctrine but maintains on diversity of cultural stances including incidents without chain of command, explicitly, without axiom that one is better than another or more advanced than the other.

Additionally, discussions on the presented matter delves into causes of Majimaji war; areas covered by Majimaji war; consequences of Majimaji war; and they pinpoint to the fact that Majimaji war was genocide. Other discussed matters include memory concerning Majimaji war; questions on repatriation including reparation of materials taken to German due to war; women's stance in Majimaji war; their recognition as heroines in the Majimaji war; Majimaji heritage resources; and Majimaji heritage landscapes.

Together with other important aspects pertaining to Majimaji war in this chapter, the chapter underscores an outstanding interpretation that Majimaji war was genocide. Such interpretation was provided by several scholars too but has not been given due prominence. This is the most important aspect explored in this chapter in providing a positive decipherment of the said war and its consequences, the atrocities. This owes to the fact that Majimaji war atrocities are purely discernible through the definition of the term genocide as offered by the 1948 United Nations Genocide Convention. Besides, most of atrocities in response to Majimaji war included the following: the colonial system legalised forced labour, imprisonment, detention in chains, imprisonment alongside confinement as well as pain, execution of local warriors and cultural genocide (ethnocide) planned to destroy lives including cultural identity of local communities. The interpretation is further ostensibly inspired as well as filtered through a theoretical lens, Afrocentricity in providing an undeniable comprehension of African realities and for that case, Majimaji war as genocide, which is a pertinent illustration of the African continent's past and present.

A review on, "Cultural Diversity in Tanzania and Germany" is presented in **Chapter Two**. For pertinent comprehension, based on socio-cultural dimensions, the chapter is organized through periods or eras experienced in Tanzania. They include interactions before colonialism, interactions during colonialism, interactions post-independence to date; and conclusions.

The chapter shows that maintained cultural diversity in Tanzania and Germany is seen from pre-colonialism, during colonialism, and post-independence up till now. It clearly highlights that the first period made possible setting up and thus, continued as well as sustained existing positive cultural diversity aspects in Tanzania and Germany. An ostensible and landmark aspect to underscore is Kiswahili language that was initiated by Arabs who incorporated words from local ethnic groups, fundamentally Bantu population groups, was further developed as well as refined by Germany missionaries who wrote Kiswahili dictionary. Outstandingly, language as a medium of culture is important for human beings' sake or livelihoods. Therefore, continued use of Kiswahili language made possible smooth dialogues and other independence (*uhuru* in Kiswahili) struggles for Tanzania that were successfully carried out by almost 120 ethnic groups in the country. Additionally, currently, Kiswahili language is the national and official language of communication that further makes people maintain peace and security in Tanzania.

Moreover, economic ventures, for instance, plantation farming of cotton and sisal established by the Germany colonial government have been and are still being carried out by the independent government. Presently, together with other additional cash crops, the country facilitates cash crop farming. Also, taxation system started by Germans is carried over and expanded to furnish government coffers as revenue for smooth running of fundamental government affairs.

Furthermore, Germans constructed infrastructure like the central railway, sea ports and numerous roads in Tanzania that are still in use for transportation of goods in the country and overseas. They were and they are still, entry points/exit points for foreign trade of Tanzania. Accordingly, the said foundations are benefitting the independent government and thus, facilitate continued socio-economic interactions not only with Germans but also with others around the world.

On the other hand, non-government actors, particularly missionaries established social services that included hospitals and schools. The health and education services have been expanded during independent Tanzania. There are regional as well as zonal referral hospitals that resulted from initial ordinary health facilities established by missionaries. Currently, health, education, good governance, democracy, gender equality, human rights as well as political matters in Tanzania (public as well as private), in all dimensions are still enjoying collaborations with the Germany government and institutions, private as well as public.

Chapter Three brings to core an aspect mostly denigrated by people for not according due recognition, heroines in war or conflict situations. In due regard, the chapter on "Heroines of Majimaji War in Tanzania from 1905 to 1907" enlightens importance of women's participation in the said war at varied capacities. The chapter provides general background; people's viewpoints on war as a masculine domain, women's participation in wars at selected places around the world, women's participation in Majimaji war, theoretical underpinning that leads to recognise Majimaji war heroines, discussions and conclusions.

Outstandingly, the chapter is centred on negative effects of colonialism, secession and patriotism that led to resistance wars around the world including Africa, in general, and Majimaji war in Tanzania, in particular. In so doing, the chapter demonstrates several heroines around the world including Africa, in general and particularly Tanzania's heroines of Majimaji war.

Additionally, the discussion in the chapter is anchored on two prominent parts. Part one presents insights into wartime statuses in gender relations. The other part presents materials by bringing into light women's participation in Majimaji war. Briefly, it is shown that some women were leaders and mobilized people for the war as well as provided other resources for the war. Equally important, *maji*, the war medicine, was managed by women who were considerable and embraced elements in ritual activities as well as in war. Besides, women were key informants as spies for men warriors in Majimaji war.

The chapter leads to a firm conclusion that women were involved in Majimaji war at varying levels – various dimensions or capacities. Their participation was extremely important in the battle. Based on their vital involvement in the said war but given little attention, it is reasonable to declare that indeed, they are unsung Majimaji war heroines.

Chapter four is centred on presenting recovered/discovered human remains, animal remains, plant remains and cultural materials that were collected, transported and stored in Germany during German colonial rule. The chapter begins with a brief description on drivers of exploration and scientific expeditions around the world followed by a short description on materials collected, transported and stored in Germany. Also, there is presentation on international measures undertaken and currently observed concerning repatriation of materials collected by persons around the world. There is discussion on some materials that have been returned to Tanzania from Germany together with questions pertaining to unreturned materials and future prospects on the matter.

It is recognized that German scientists led the way in scientific research undertakings in many disciplines in Tanzania. Notable disciplines included geology, geography, anthropology and many others. Besides, during colonial rule in Tanzania, particularly during conflicts and Majimaji war, they collected remains of human skeletal materials – mostly skulls. As a result, they collected human skeletal materials from extant species and also, they collected proto-human species (fossils) that are extinct that mostly included non-human objects. Due to some reasons including scientific and technical ability, they shipped such remains to Germany.

There are some noted initiatives by leaders of the United Republic of Tanzania and Germany Federal Government aimed at repatriation of materials taken from Tanzania to Germany. So far there are no registered measures of repatriation of such materials. Such position leads to looming questions to the said collected materials from Tanzania. This is due to the fact that very few materials have been returned to Tanzania. Thus, the following questions are at the centre-stage: due to unclear positions on what was taken and what was not taken, what materials were shipped to German during colonial rule? Such question is tied together on whereabouts of many likely unknown human, cultural objects including other material remains stored in Germany - what is the way forward to their repatriation? What is their fate? Who are in possession of such materials? Are they in custody of academic institutions, public and private (universities, museums) or private individuals? Are there scientific collaborations between German and Tanzanian scientists along with technicians in dealing with repatriation of materials taken from Tanzania during German colonial rule?

Something must be done to repatriate materials taken from Tanzania to Germany. The stance is based on the fact that although there is no international legal commitment to return cultural materials acquired during the colonial period, their repatriation is a moral duty and it owes logic of commitment to repair long-ago injustices. Accordingly, the undertaking is possible through wisdom, negotiation and agreement. Besides, based on the fact that many are not known where they are stored and by whom in Germany, the desired measures should involve establishment or identification of an institution or institutions to supervise the demands. Additionally, there could be measures such as voluntary donations or restitutions, while other moves could be mediation or arbitration. However, the latter measures can lead to problems that must be carefully observed. For instance, judges as well as lawyers must be ready to face complex practical including procedural undertakings so as to identify the applicable law/laws but there is no guarantee for perfect and/or smooth execution of the undertakings.

Importantly, as a window of hope, the two countries have firm/strong diplomatic ties with cooperation between government bodies, as well as private entities for socio-economic developments. There is government will on both sides, Federal Government of Germany and United Republic of Tanzania, on aspirations to repatriate as well as undertake reparation for materials collected by Germans during their colonial rule. Therefore, there is a ray hope for such positive measures.

Chapter Five presents on German built heritage for continued use for socio-economic development in Tanzania. The chapter sets up on a brief description showing that Tanganyika (now mainland Tanzania) was under German colonial rule. It is followed by rationale for presenting the chapter. The chapter has the following sections: Infrastructure for Socio-Economic Services; Economic Ventures; Establishment and Development of Transport Infrastructure; Establishment of Trade Centres; Establishment of Social Services; Kiswahili Language; Research and Development; Discussion; and Future Prospects.

Built heritage resources developed during German rule are still in use and they are still being restored, maintained as well as conserved. Importantly, such measures, to a great extent, keep their historic fabric, value, authenticity and as a result, their continued use permit activation of their potential as dynamic resources that serve the government (for inherited assets) and local people's needs including government use. The built heritage resources include tangible cultural as well as intangible cultural heritage assets that are in use by offering social services such as education, health care, worship and Kiswahili language use, while others are for trade via transportation networks like railway system, roads, ports/harbours and customs ware houses.

The chapter furnishes materials by using a pertinent cognitive frame of reference, namely, Afrocentricity Theory. This is based on the safe argument that the extant German built heritage in Tanzania is unquestionably important to the country's current use for socio-economic development. The position is crucial due to the fact that the said built heritage does not denigrate Tanzania's stance on its continued use and maintenance.

Germany rule established settlements in terms of buildings that were important set up and expansion of some clusters into towns. They were also important centres for governance from the capital to other low governance levels in the country. Also, they developed road as well as railways infrastructure and cash crop cultivation including social services for socio-economic development. Such heritage resources were crucial for later and current socio-economic development for independent Tanzania. The independent Tanzania benefits a lot from such ventures established and developed by German rulers.

Additionally, commencement of agricultural activities for cash crops for export was important by then and they are still important for the country's socio-economic development. The country is still using and it has improved further infrastructure, for example, the central railway from Dar es Salaam to Kigoma and the other Dar es Salaam, Tanga to Moshi line are still operative. The road network established by the German authority was a stepping stone for further development of roads in the country. The country has been and is still building as well as maintaining roads by extending from already set up roads by German authority.

Established social services during German rule such as schools and healthcare facilities are still beneficial to the country. Schools that were established under German rule acted as points of departure for further development of education in the country. In fact, the early teachings at elementary level that also encompassed trainings in technical education are still beneficial, to date. Trainings involved use of medium of instruction, besides, Germany, Kiswahili was used. Importantly, German scholars were the first to develop Kiswahili language by publishing books such as the first Kiswahili dictionary, grammar and other language books. They made Kiswahili the official language and medium of instruction in the schools, both private (owned by missionaries) and government owned.

Some ports that were in use for maritime trade were taken over by German rulers. They were improved. The ports including the link with the railway line were and are still serving for import and export of commodities. Additionally, with the ship, M.V. Liemba still plying Lake Tanganyika waters (though intermittently stops for overhaul) is a great assert for the country's socio-economic development. All such establishments and eventual developments have facilitated growth including sprawl of areas into big urban centres that have also increased their socio-economic ventures at various dimensions in the country.

Furthermore, establishment of dock yard and Customs Department by German rulers was extremely important later for the independent country's socio-economic development. The systematic cargo handling for import and export established by German authority paved the way for the independent country to continuously give a facelift to such facilities around the country. Besides, they were linked with the railway, particularly end points like Kigoma in eastern Lake Tanganyika shores such that currently, they are important centres for import and export businesses together with link to neighbouring countries like Democratic Republic of Congo and Burundi.

Additionally, set up of Customs Department meant systematic establishment of taxation system in the country by German authority for import and export of commodities. The country, as of mid-1990s, in its continued redress of the taxation system that includes revenue collection for import and export businesses, established the Tanzania Revenue Authority (TRA). All such moves are possible due to the fact that for over a hundred years ago, the country has been with taxation system for local businesses along with import and export of commodities.

Kiswahili language is still the official medium of instruction in primary schools. Similar to unification of people by posting Kiswahili conversant officials around the country together with eventual spread of using Kiswahili, it united people and it was used during non-violent independence struggles by local people in Tanzania. Of utmost importance, due to such developments, in 1963, Kiswahili became the national language. Up to now, Kiswahili is the medium of instruction in elementary schools. Moreover, there are degree courses in Kiswahili at universities in the country. Further developments in Kiswahili in the early 1970s, led to government order that Kiswahili language as the official and government language in all government communications. The order is still in force, to date.

It is undeniable that built infrastructure by German authorities in Tanzania is still important to the current and future generations for socio-economic development. Such built heritage documents and preserves the historic significance including potential of the country. It still offers many socio-economic benefits to the country.

Collaborative measures for improvement of social services with German authority and private entities are still important avenues to be considered and carried out sustainably. All moves are possible due to the fact that the two countries (Tanzania and Germany) have long standing diplomatic ties. They have been and they are still collaborating for Tanzania's socio-economic development for many decades. There are many areas of operations that range from health care, education, agriculture, economic cooperation and social matters. German rule in Tanzania has many benefits and they are currently carried out through several collaborative measures between the United Republic of Tanzania and the German Federal Government including developing partners in German. Importantly, most of the collaborations are beneficial not only to Tanzania but also to Germany. Therefore, such benefits must be sustainably carried out by the two state parties.

Chapter Six deals with the topic of the responsibilities of Scientists, Lecturers and Politicians of German descent to work about the Tanzanian German-Past and the Genocide against the members of the Majimaji Movement 1905 – 1907. The practices of silencing, missing knowledge and a lack of interest have to be changed in active research, in reading the research results of Tanzanian Researchers and in a practice of listening to Tanzanian voices from Tanzania and in Germany. Also the work of Tanzanian scientists and activists in German Diaspora has to be recognized as pan-African transnational approach and important scientific contribution.

Ways of cooperation between researchers with Tanzanian and German descent shall be established to make pressure especially on German politicians stopping their denial and hypocrisy concerning the Genocide Germans committed in Tanzania, concerning the stolen human and animal remains, the stolen art and cultural objects.

After more than 117 years the German Government has officially to confess in a government solution (Bundestagsresolution): Germany has committed a Genocide 1905-1907 against the Members of the Majimaji Movement in Tanzania, we have to pay for Reparation and there will be the Repatriation of all stolen objects.

In schools and universities, lecturers and students have intensely work about theses themes in cooperation with non-government organizations and lecturers and scientists with Tanzanian descent. Like the Herero and Nama say: Everything about us without us is against us.

This work is the result of the cooperation between Tanzanian and German Universities and Researchers and we hope to inspire you and to bring the discussions on a higher level.

Sakina Faru, Charles Sanaane, Claus Melter

CHAPTER ONE

IN MEMORY OF GENOCIDE AGAINST MEMBERS OF MAJIMAJI MOVEMENT IN TANZANIA FROM 1905 TO 1907

Dr. Sakina Faru

General Overview

This chapter under the theme, "In memory of genocide against members of the Majimaji Movement in Tanzania from 1905 to 1907" provides a review of other scholars' works in various disciplines including History, Literature, Historical Archaeology and Ethnoarchaeology. The review is based on proponents' research endeavours at various dimensions that include historical data sets, principally from unpublished historical sources (notably, archival materials, oral accounts and published data sets). Different aspects to memorise, discuss, functionalise or to deny and minimise genocide against members of the Majimaji Movement are provided. In contextualising the chapter, it forms the following parts: the setting; discussion; and concluding remarks.

Importantly, this chapter is presented because there are many interpretations about Majimaji war based on a fair amount of research endeavours but the facts seem to provide room for many controversial questions (Koponen, 2010). For example, the manner the revolts were called in the beginning by German colonists was Majimaji rebellion, while during struggles for independence and after independence, the battle was called and is still called, Majimaji war. Atrocities and thus, consequences of the war are variously interpreted with some calling genocide to both Africans and Germans, whereas others refrain from mentioning the said inhuman undertakings. Such stance is due to existing accounts including some of the primary sources that furnish a lee way for questioning their correctness as well as relevance (*ibid.*).

There is no doubt about meticulous presentation of the chronology of events of Majimaji from their start to eventual containment but many questions concerning Majimaji loom around. Koponen (2010: 2 and 3) brings to attention that,

> "Historians will recognize this to a great extent as a source problem: the sources from which the facts concerning Maji Maji have been extracted are relatively few and of questionable reliability, as almost all of them have a particular axe to grind. The German colonial records, outwardly the most extensive, most detailed, and most reliable sources, document and date meticulously every 'disturbance' that came to the knowledge of the colonialists as well as the German countermeasures to these. Yet not only is such a view culturally very thin but the Germans also were badly out of touch with events and often disagreed among themselves. They simply did not know much about what was going on; indeed, had they be better informed, the rebellion might never have reached the proportion it did. Missionary sources are, in this case, inferior to colonialist ones. Missionaries, while ostensibly living near the people, could not possibly have known what was going on among the rebellious 'heathens' before disquieting rumours inevitably reached them on the eve of the imminent attack. Their accounts reflect the concerns of survival of a beleaguered righteous minority and cannot be expected to provide a realistic assessment of the nature of forces threatening their very existence. Oral sources, for their part, originate from research undertaken somewhat fitfully in three broad cycles in the colonial and postcolonial periods. Their great merit, of course, is that they provide the opportunity to hear the voice of those actually involved on the African side; whether they actually accomplish this is another thing. The malleability of oral communication and its susceptibility to the 'contaminating' influence of later written and other authoritative accounts and events is well known; and the further they are from the actual events the

less original information they contain and the more they tend to conflate and telescope several historical processes into one. Oral memory is also highly localized; the same events can be remembered and assessed very differently in geographically nearby places. Yet the problem goes way beyond the sources. The sources have to do with 'simple facts' and historians are basically interested in 'institutional facts', or 'interpretations', to use the vernacular term. The basic requirement for judging the interpretations is, of course, that the interpretation concerned fits the known 'facts', or data, better than its rivals do and makes better sense of what factually seems to have happened. This might be called the 'knowledge' or cognitive requirement. But it also goes the other way around. What is taken as a fact and what is not is dependent also on our interpretative framework, and interpretations are based not only on facts. They also must resonate with the intellectual or political views – whether they are popular or academic, and whether we call them narratives or paradigms - prevalent among the interpreters at that particular time and place. This may be called the 'power' or instrumental requirement. Whereas an interpretation can emerge and survive for some time relying mainly on one or the other of these sets of requirements, in the long run it is the interpretation that fulfils both conditions best that carries the day. For Maji Maji, it is no coincidence that colonial and nationalist interpretations in their solidity are like mirror images, and both have now been challenged by more fragmented postcolonial or postmodern interpretations."

1.1 The Setting

1.1.0 Definitions of terms and concepts

This part presents definitions including notes of essential terms and concepts. They include the following: Majimaji; genocide; Afrocentricity; and renaming of Majimaji in Tanzanian context.

1.1.1 Majimaji

In Kiswahili literature, the word "… is written as one word as it is pronounced Majimaji" (Rushohora, 2015: 5; De Juan, 2016: 300). Nonetheless, some scholars, for example, Mwaifuge (2014), Koponen (2010), Mapunda (2010) and Becker (2004) write the term as two separate bodies (Maji Maji), whereas, for instance, Moffett (1958) as well as Schaller (2008) write the word with hyphen MajiMaji. On the other hand, LeGall (2020), Rushohora and Silayo (2019) as well as Ebner (2009) used the word as a single term, "Majimaji." In this chapter, based on Kiswahili language syntax where compounds are written as one word, the term is used as a single word, Majimaji.

In regard to Majimaji war, the word *maji* refers to war medicine that was employed to immunise, cure or protect Majimaji warriors, their families and properties during the war (Rushohora, 2015; Larson, 2010). Notably, even though *maji* means water in Kiswahili, as a cult, *maji* is not identical with water, it was a war medicine in liquid form because the said medicine had water including other herbs that was applied by bathing, sprinkling or spraying Majimaji warriors (Rushohora and Silayo, 2019; Gwassa, 2005).

Accordingly, as a war agentive and symbolic aspect (Rushohora, 2017), people's minds were strengthened by belief in *maji* that was alleged to bestow invulnerability against German bullets (Larson, 2010). Other significant agents in Majimaji war included diviners' residences and shrines (*op cit*.). Even though Kinjekitile Ngwale is reported to have had been the primary divine leader with his residence being the centre for traditional rites, "… communities subscribed to their own religious leaders and shrines during the Majimaji…" because "… Kinjekitile was arrested and killed shortly before the beginning of the war… the war spread over a too large an area with differences in culture and religious practices" (Rushohora, 2017: 22). In due regard, all through, the war was directed by religious dogma such that spiritual leaders including shrines were important places over Majimaji landscape (*ibid*.: 22). Accordingly, *maji* medicine was an important instrument among war agents thereby paved for naming the war Majimaji (Rushohora, 2017). Notably, historians referred to *maji* medicine to be with influential and symbolic effective ritual deeds that guaranteed imperviousness as well as means to collect people together into a mass movement (Monson, 2010: 36; Gwassa, 1969).

1.1.2 Genocide

According to Odello and Piotr (2020: xiii), Raphael Lemkin was the first to formulate the concept of genocide during the Second World War. Subsequent to "… the end of the war, and while the atrocities committed against millions of civilians were coming to light, the United Nations committed itself to adopting a legal document that would define certain types of crimes that could be prevented and punished under international law" (Odello and Piotr, 2020: xiii). It is recorded that The 1948 Convention on the Prevention and Punishment of the Crime of Genocide was the outcome of Lemkin's endeavours to provide a legal definition of crime he had previously identified as an international crime in his writings (Odello and Piotr, (2020: xiii). His original definition encompassed an array of acts that would affect certain groups and could lead to destruction or wiping out targeted groups (*ibid.*: xiii).

Currently, the definition of genocide, which corresponds to Lemkin's main suppositions, is in the United Nations Convention on Prevention and Punishment of the Crime of Genocide that was adopted in Paris, France on 9th December, 1948 (*ibid.*: 8). Article I of the Convention declares that states party to it confirmed that genocide, whether committed in a time of peace or in a time of war, is a crime under international law, which they undertake to prevent and to punish (*ibid.*: 8).

According to the Convention,

> "Genocide means any of the following acts committed with intent to destroy, in whole or in part, a national, ethnical, racial or religious group, as such: a. Killing members of the group; b. Causing serious bodily or mental harm to members of the group; c. Deliberately inflicting on the group conditions of life calculated to bring about its physical destruction in whole or in part; d. Imposing measures intended to prevent births within the group; e. Forcibly transferring children of the group to another group. The above definition was the result of a negotiating process and reflected the compromise reached among the UN member states" (*ibid.*: 9).

Nonetheless, there are challenges in implementation of the Genocide Convention (*ibid.*: 10). In spite of challenges in implementing the Genocide

Convention, the same definition was incorporated in "… the Rome Statute of the International Criminal Court (Article 6), and was also part of the jurisdiction of *ad hoc* and hybrid courts, including the International Criminal Tribunal for the Former Yugoslavia and the International Criminal Tribunal for Rwanda" (*ibid.*: 10). Notably, the Convention was ratified by 152 UN member states "… and the International Court of Justice (ICJ) has continually stated that the Convention embodies principles that are part of general customary international law. The ICJ also stated that the prohibition of genocide is a *ius cogens* norm of international law (peremptory norm) and that no derogation from it is allowed" (*ibid.*: 10).

Pertaining to prevention of genocide around the world, it must be underscored that the Genocide Convention does not exactly explain nature as well as extent of prevention commitment (*ibid.*: 11). As informed based on Lemkin's formulation, his focus was on the desire to punish perpetrators (*ibid.*: 11). As a result, states were indebted to set up domestic law to permit them to be found guilty of genocide, apart from "… whether they are constitutionally responsible members of the government, public officials, or private individuals (Article 4.31). It is not explained what other actions should be taken by states to prevent genocide" (*ibid.*: 11).

1.1.3 Afrocentricity

Afrocentricity was formulated and developed as a result of Pan-Africanism and Black Nationalism (Shockley & Frederick, 2010; Watson, 2015: 47). Notably, the late Kwame Nkrumah – organizer of the Fifth Pan African Congress and former president of Ghana – first employed the term "Afrocentricity" in the 1960s, before it was popularized in the 1980s by Prof. Molefi Kete Asante (Watson, 2015: 47).

Presently, "… Asante is known for developing Afrocentricity into a social and theoretical framework" (Khokholkova, 2016; Watson, 2015: 47). Therefore, he is one of leading proponents of Afrocentric theory [and regarded as father as well as esteemed theorist of Afrocentricity (Anderson, 2012; Khokholkova, 2016)], Prof. Molefi Kete Asante (1987), defined that,

> "Afrocentricity is the most complete philosophical totalization of the African being at-the-center of his or her existence. It is not merely an artistic or literary movement. Not only is it an individual or collective quest for authenticity, but it is

above all the total use of the method to affect psychological, political, social, cultural, and economic change. The Afrocentric idea is beyond decolonizing the mind."

Thus, the first definition of Afrocentricity was provided by Asante that meant African-centered as situating of African ideals at the center of any analysis that involves African culture and behavior (Bangura, 2012). It is argued that even though Prof. Diop did not use the term Afrocentricity, his master piece research endeavours laid the foundation for Afrocentric research, notably, in his work of 1974 titled "The African Origin of Civilization: Myth or Reality" (*ibid.*: 109).

In short, as a framework, Afrocentricity is defined as re-centering African agency from objects to participants in history (Khokholkova, 2016: 47). Currently, Afrocentricity as a framework confronts hegemony as Asante (1998: 4) argued that, "Many today find it difficult to stop view European/American culture as the center of the social universe" (Watson, 2015: 47). Khokholkova submitted Asante's (1993: 1) formulation that,

> "Afrocentricity's role is to disrupt the hegemonic centrality of Europe into a more diversified outlook. Because Eurocentric ethos has been widely accepted for so long, '[people] often assumed that their' 'objectivity,' a kind of collective subjectivity of European culture, should be the measure by which the world marches."

In his later publication, "An Afrocentric Manifesto: Toward an African Renaissance," Asante split his paradigm into several branches and defined that,

> "Afrocentricity is a paradigmatic intellectual perspective that privileges African agency within the context of African history and culture trans-continentally and trans-generationally. This means that the quality of location is essential to any analysis that involves African culture and behavior whether literary or economic, whether political or cultural. In this regard, it is the crystallization of a critical perspective on facts" (Asante, 2007: 2).

Important to note is that Afrocentricity should not be

> "… confused with Afrocentrism, which is negatively labeled by some scholars … as 'Eurocentrism with Black face,' 'Black

nationalism,' 'Ethnic pride' or whatever designed to combat the destructive consequences of universal racism and cultural imperialism on African people. Without taking the risk of plugging into unnecessary and unproductive debates, the main challenge for the Afrocentrist is to provide a different interpretation of the African realities, a new visualization of the continent's past and present so that to liberate the minds of the ignorant or miseducated masses" (Rodrigue, 2020: 12).

Notably, Afrocentric paradigm was developed into Afrocentric Theory. Afrocentric Theory was first developed in the United States of America (USA) in the 1980s, through Asante's book "Afrocentricity: The Theory of Social Change" (Khokholkova, 2016). According to Bangura (2012: 112), many advocates contributed to formation and recognition of Afrocentricity but the following four were the most prominent in advancement of Afrocentricity: W. E. B. Du Bois, Cheikh Anta Diop, Kwame Nkrumah and Gerald Massey.

Bangura (2012: 117, 118) submits that Afrocentricity has major theories and concepts that form the basis of the discipline (Africology). They include the following: i) Matriarchal Origins Theory; ii) Two-Cradle Theory; iii) Analogical Symbols Theory; iv) Kawaida; and The African Code (*ibid.*: 117, 118).

Concerning Matriarchal Theory, it was argued that the majority of African civilizations before the spread "… of Christianity and Islam were matriarchal in structure with women being shown high levels of respect" (*ibid.*: 117). Pertaining to Two-Cradle Theory, it was held that Blacks in Africa and Whites in Eurasia dwelt in two separate localities or cradles that portrayed their physical features, cultures, histories as well as cognitive styles (*ibid.*: 117). Nonetheless, the theory was contested and thus, discredited by many scientists due to new evidences that point to Africa as the exclusive cradle of civilization (*ibid.*: 117). On Analogical Symbols Theory, it was submitted that African symbolism was "… based on finding similarities between things and representing those things incomprehensible, abstraction, by that which is comprehensible" (*ibid:.* 117).

Kawaida as the framework was conjured up and formulated

"… as a philosophy in the midst of the liberation struggle of the 1960s as an emancipatory philosophy dedicated to Cultural Revolution, radical social change, and bringing good in the world. Kawaida was shaped by its focus on culture and community as the basis and building blocks for any real movement for the liberation of African people everywhere" (*ibid.*: 118).

On the other hand, Kawaida is a continuing "... synthesis of African thought and practice in constant exchange with the world, asking questions and seeking answers to central and enduring concerns of the African and human community" (*ibid.*: 118). Finally, The African Code is a conception "... in Pan-Africanism that stresses unity through diversity based upon the seven key principles of Kwanza delineated by Maulana Karenga: (1) Umoja—Unity; (2) Kujichagulia—Self-determination; (3) Ujima—Collective Work and Responsibility; (4) Ujamaa—Cooperative Economics; (5) Nia—Purpose; (6) Kuumba— Creativity; and (7) Imani—Faith. The African Code acts as an intersection of a global Pan-African ethos for unity through diversity" (*ibid.*: 118).

Kwanza has been translated into more than 30 languages and works "... as a non-political, non-religious cultural commonality for African people seeking self-determination everywhere. The African Code employs the Ge'ez alphabet and treats Kiswahili as the official Pan-African language and, subsequently, Ge'ez as an African script to replace all forms of Latin to write all African languages" (*ibid.*: 118).

According to Bangura (2012: 118), the presented theories and concepts assist to direct research endeavours in Afrocentricity. The stance was based on an argument that the theories "... define that which is African; and by doing this, they establish a means of differentiating between that which is African and anything else" (*ibid.*: 118).

Nonetheless, aspects to note include the fact that Afrocentricity, even though heavily grounded in research undertakings, got strong disagreements. Several proponents were opposed to Afrocentricity, for example, Ravitch (1990), Schlesinger (1998), and Lefkowitz (1997) criticized claims of Afrocentricity as well as disagreed with Pan-Africanists such as Molefi Asante, John Henrik Clarke, and Théophile Obenga (Watson, 2015: 48). Moreover, several African American researchers, for instance, Henry Louis Gates (1991) and Tunde Adeleke (2009) criticised Afrocentric theory (*ibid.*: 48).

Watson (2015: 48) submitted, for example,

> "Gates (1991) skeptically dismisses Afrocentricity's utility in general and asserts in a widely published Newsweek article

entitled 'Beware of the New Pharaohs.' Gates (1991) claimed that, '… too many people still regard African American studies primarily as a way to rediscover a lost cultural identity – or invent one that never quite existed' (p. 47). Adeleke (2009) asserts that Afrocentricity is essentialist and monolithic. However, the very basis of Afrocentricity dispels theories that perpetuate essentialist and monolithic views of history."

In response to such criticisms that point to pertinent use of the theoretical stance, Watson (2015: 48) provided Asante's (2003: 268) rebuttal that,

> "Afrocentrists have never opposed any racial group or supported any type of discrimination… true Afrocentrist[s] cannot support any racist doctrine but must insist on diversity of cultural positions and experiences without hierarchy – that is, without saying one is better than another or more advanced than the other…. In response to its opposition, it is important to note that European hegemony – not any specific persons or racial group – are the premise of Afrocentricity…"

1.1.4 Renaming of Majimaji in Tanzanian context

Majimaji was initially called by German administrators, for instance, Götzen a 'rebellion,' a 'revolt' or an 'uprising' based on criteria used by other parts of the world (Gwassa, 1969; Rushohora, 2017: 19). Such criteria distinguish divergences from ambushes, scuffles, unrests or riots, mass murders or other types (*ibid.*). Accordingly, based on many expressions, inclined through nationalism thereby regarding Majimaji as the early seeds sown for struggles for independence and the like, particularly a few years after the country was independent, Tanzania regards Majimaji as a war that was an active resistance and real battle that occurred in the country (Rushohora, 2017: 19; Lawi, 2009).

1.2 Discussion

It is reported that the uprising first broke in Lindi and Kilwa districts, southeastern Tanzania whereby Wangindo communities were among the first to revolt against German oppression (Greiner, 2022). The war was not only waged against the colonial state's representatives but also it involved damage to the physical landscape, for instance, they sabotaged kilometre marker stones along the constructed Kilwa road that previously involved people's forced labour (*ibid.*). Of special note is that the war ended in August, 1907 following gradual suppression (*ibid.*).

This section furnishes discussion on the following aspects: causes of Majimaji war; areas covered by Majimaji war; consequences of Majimaji war; genocide or not genocide; memory pertaining to Majimaji war; repatriation as well as reparation; women and heroines in the Majimaji war; Majimaji heritage resources; and Majimaji heritage landscapes.

For some sub-sections, the discussion uses Afrocentricity as an analytical lens for critical voyaging following Asante's assertion that Afrocentricity is African-centered thereby paves the way in situating of African ideals at the center of any analysis that involves African culture and behaviour (see Bangura, 2012). Moreover, employing Afrocentricity is strengthened from Watson's (2015: 48) submission of Asante's (2003: 268) position,

> "Afrocentrists have never opposed any racial group or supported any type of discrimination… true Afrocentrist[s] cannot support any racist doctrine but must insist on diversity of cultural positions and experiences without hierarchy – that is, without saying one is better than another or more advanced than the other…"

1.2.0   Causes of Majimaji war

Various authors have submitted about causes of Majimaji war but it has to be noted that they were diverse and "no single cause can explain the war to the fullest and the war was not spontaneous" (Gwassa, 1973: 10; Rushohora, 2015: 119). It must be underscored that drives to participate in the Majimaji war varied from region to region (Sunseri, 2010: 141, Rushohora, 2015: 202). Generally, causes of Majimaji war included the following: forced cotton cultivation as well as rubber extraction; heavy taxation; and compulsory labour as well as harassment in road construction.

1.2.1 Forced cotton cultivation and rubber extraction

Colonial projects were sources of numerous resistances in Africa and they were accompanied by land alienation, forced labour and taxation that were unknown in the African context (Rushohora, 2015: 202). Likewise, in Tanzania, several projects were established by colonialists that included set up of agriculture, trade and industries to exploit raw materials (*ibid.*: 202).

De Juan's (2016) analysis uncovered that grievances due to forced and later on intensification of cotton cultivation partially led to Majimaji war but expansion of extraction into the then rewarding rubber trade threatened local leaders' political as well as economic authority and eventually, led to widespread anti-state violence. Thus, such measures created to local people's loss of control over the economy as well as the environment (Greiner, 2022).

It is argued that each state's survival depends on its ability to extract resources that permit it to uphold as well as enlarge its authority (De Juan, 2016). Accordingly, extractive undertakings further strongly influence state to population relations because they comprise a primary involvement in social life as well as impinge on local political and economic structures thereby create an economic trouble (De Juan, 2016).

In the country, the said extractive undertakings had their genesis and growth through German colonial projects established as private enterprises whereby in 1884, Carl Peters established the Society for German Colonialisation [later renamed the Deutsch-Ostafrikanische Gesellschaft (DOAG) translated as German East-African Society, De Juan, 2016]. It is reported that Peters' ambitions included to acquire colonies for Germany, improve the international position of the German Reich and secure personal profit (*ibid.*).

For several years, the DOAG expanded its territory as well as its activities and in 1888, such progression paved the way for violent interruptions by already Arabs established along the coastal areas of Tanzania and was named as 'Arab Revolt' (Iliffe, 1979; De Juan, 2016). In 1890, on behalf of DOG, the Governor, Bismarck, intervened and dispatched a military mission that defeated the rebellion (De Juan, 2016). Such intervention led to transfer of all administrative functions from the DOAG to the imperial government (Iliffe, 1979; De Juan, 2016). Accordingly, German colonial state-building was marked by considerable internal contradictions (De Juan, 2016). Due to limitation of manpower including resources to administer and manage across a large expanse of the territory already occupied by Germans, local leaders became middle persons for the government and at the same time, they established modes of both direct rule and indirect rule (Iliffe, 1979; De Juan, 2016).

Colonial administrative statuses across the country led to varied nature of grievances and as a result, there were uprisings due to forced labour in plantations. Accordingly, a "… cotton plantation at Nandete was the site of the symbolic origin of the Majimaji war. According to Mr. Verimond Kipengele, it was in this plantation the Majimaji war was declared" (Rushohora, 2015: 202). The cotton plantation was reproduction of analogous plantations as well as colonial projects across southern Tanzania (*ibid.*). As a result, in all areas where Majimaji war was fought, people had colonial projects or systems they desired to resist (*ibid.*). Furthermore, in 1903 in Liwale, abolishment of trade in wild rubber and its replacement by obliged cultivation in rubber as well as cotton plantations sparked for Majimaji war occurrence (Larson, 2010: 100; Rushohora, 2015: 202).

1.2.2 Heavy taxation

According to Koponen (2010: 18), people were aggrieved by taxation system due to colonial involvement that structured a plethora of taxes, decrees and regulations. Additionally, disgruntlement, clearly engendered by taxation, particularly money tax usually accompanied with cruel methods of its collection elevated people's resistance (*ibid.*: 18). Accordingly, "… when tax payment was demanded in cash, it forced people to intensify the collection of rubber or copal or to engage in wage work as porters or estate labourers, or alternatively, to settle tax obligations labouring for the local boma" (*ibid.*: 18).

Besides, as it is shown in sub-section on compulsory labour, tax was forced to people so as to cater for road construction and those who did not manage to pay tax, were obliged to work in road construction (Greiner, 2022). A new tax order assisted Germans to acquire a huge amount of cheap labour needed for various construction sites (*ibid.*). That was a tax reform whereby the usual tax on huts (households) that was paid in kind was to be replaced by a personal tax due in cash (Bachmann, 2018). All such measures were desired to facilitate colonial government works including road works, "… from April 1898 on, the government introduced a so-called hut tax of 3 to 12 rupees to be paid per annum in either cash or produce by every house and hut owner in the 'pacified' parts of the colony" (*ibid.*). Consequently, people revolted with violence against forced taxation.

1.2.3 Compulsory labour and harassment in road construction

Like any other government, colonial or otherwise, the colonial government was involved in development as well as maintenance of infrastructure, particularly roads but such ventures were among causes of Majimaji uprisings. It is informed that in 1897, the new governor, Eduard von Liebert "… made road construction a primary task of the colonial administration" (Greiner, 2022). Some projects involved reworking of some existing structures, while others were newly planned (*ibid.*). Such construction works started in 1897, for example, from Kilwa and Lindi to the interior in south-eastern Tanzania, road works in Dar es Salaam resumed, while new roads were planned between Lake Nyasa in southern Tanzania and Lake Tanganyika as well as between Tabora and Mwanza along Lake Victoria (*ibid.*).

In order to execute road construction works, a new tax order helped the Germans get huge amounts of cheap labour necessary for construction sites (*ibid.*). It was anticipated that the undertaking to clear close by roads was a compliment from local residents and at the same time, added road works were to be carried out by tax defaulters who were obliged to work for the colonial government (*ibid.*). For example, such scheme was employed by police commander (Eugen Styx) on the road works from Lindi to Masasi in south-eastern Tanzania whereby one hundred tax workers for a day were employed and replaced by the hundred workers of the next village the moment they had worked off the village's tax debts (*ibid.*). Nonetheless, such method did not prevent non-compliance by people forced into road works and people opposed such measures as illustrated, for example, in Kisaki in eastern central Tanzania whereby they opposed his command (*ibid.*). They claimed that "are we the slaves or debtors of Europeans? Each day taxes and public works, why oh why?" (*ibid.*).

A similar pattern was challenged to work for the colonial state by people across the country. For example, in Tabora district (away from Majimaji locations), a group of villagers refused to work in such road works, a situation that led the local authority to dispatch a military mission in May 1899 (*ibid.*). In the same year, non-compliance was equally echoed in Moshi, Kilimanjaro region (though away from Majimaji war areas) whereby a great majority of people paid their taxes in labour and thus, they questioned because they thought that such measures made them feel like slaves (*ibid.*). According to local people's mindsets, recruitment or mobilization without compensation stunningly resembled slavery (*ibid.*).

As a result, the colonial state machinery responded to such open revolt with violence, for example, in spring 1901, through a military campaign against people of Kisaki in Morogoro rural district, Morogoro region, but they did not thwart the clear people's disregard of their orders (*ibid.*). Further infrastructure developments were planned including railways construction and thus, required labour to be drawn from tax. As a result, in March, 1905, a new tax of three rupees, the currency used by then, was to be paid by males in construction of infrastructure (*ibid.*). All together, it was ordered,

> "… that any man could be forced to work in road construction for free – in addition to the existing road maintenance duties. This burden added more tension to the already smouldering conflicts in German East Africa. In April 1905, the Dar es Salaam-based weekly Deutsch-Ostafrikanische Zeitung warned that in the Kilwa district frustration grew among the Ngindo people: 'Quite apart from the unpaid cleaning of the *barabara* – a practice common to all districts – the new construction of large, public thoroughfares seems a risky step that may serve to embitter the Wangindo because it conflicts with their rubber collection and field preparation [activities]'. In mid-1905, the Maji Maji War broke out in southern Tanzania, from where it spread over large parts of the colony" (*ibid.*).

1.2.4 Wildlife ordinances

Besides forced cultivation and other forced labour measures in areas that triggered Majimaji war, the colonial administration enforced ordinances and rules for people's abolishment of activities in exploiting natural resources. For instance, the colonial government enforced restrictions on hunting, in particular, it banned hunting wild animals by nets (Koponen, 2010: 18).

1.3 Areas covered by Majimaji war

Violent resistance against German rule erupted with varying intensity across most parts of the territory (Greiner, 2022; De Juan, 2016; Rushohora,

2015). There is evidence that Lindi and Kilwa districts were areas where the uprising first broke out in the country (Greiner, 2022). They were areas where Wangindo communities were among the first to revolt against German oppression such that they fought against the state's representatives and the physical landscape (*ibid.*) For the landscape, for instance, they sabotaged kilometre marker stones along Kilwa to Liwale road that they had been forced to build before (*ibid.*). The Majimaji war ended in August 1907 (*ibid.*).

Majimaji war spread to other parts of the country organised as well as spearheaded by both men and women warriors in fighting against Germans (Shiraz, 1984; Rushohora & Kurmann, 2017; Gregory, 2020). The warriors were drawn from about 20 different ethnic groups that included Wamatumbi, Wagindo, Wapogoro, Wamwera, Wayao and Wangoni, just to mention a few (Rushohora, 20015). Majimaji war was led by leaders, namely, Ndimi Omcheka, Ngurumbale Mandai and Mtemangani of Kilwa, Kinjekitile Ngwale of Ngarambe-Rufiji, Chief Chabruma, and Nduna of Songea against German colonial rule (Rushohora, 20015; Gregory, 2020). Outstandingly, ethnic groups in the southern areas of the country had a lot of resistances, for example, Wapogoro (Morogoro region) in 1898, Wanyakyusa (Mbeya region) in 1989 and Wamatengo (Ruvuma region) in 1902 (Rushohora, 2015: 43).

The southern part of the country was the bigger starting place of dynamic Majimaji war than other parts (Rushohora, 2015: 43). It is reported, for instance, in 1890, the Wayao leader, Chief Machemba, resisted against Germans led by Commander Herman von Wissmann and upon his defeat, he fled to Mozambique (Iliffe, 1979; Rushohora, 2015: 43).

Moreover, before outbreak of Majimaji war in 1905, there was one of the furthermost challenges that were strongly raised by Chief Mkwawa of Uhehe in Iringa who was defeated by Germans in 1894, but before in 1891, his army killed the German Commander, Zelewski and almost wiped out soldiers (Iliffe, 1979; Rushohora, 2015: 43). However, in 1898, to evade Germans' arrest as well as execution, Chief Mkwawa committed suicide (Iliffe, 1979: 108; Rushohora, 2015: 43).

1.3.0 Consequences of Majimaji war

Around the world, many-sided historical tremors, for example, Majimaji war, not only had numerous causes but also they had many consequences (Koponen, 2010: 23). Accordingly, it was remarked that there should be consideration that consequences of Majimaji should be viewed through ensuing developments (*ibid.*: 24). Majimaji war had the following consequences: devastation and depopulation; internal changes; changes from extractive to developmental colonialism; and development as well as neglect. They are presented in subsequent sub-sections.

1.3.1   Devastation and depopulation

An immediate observation from Majimaji war led to see "… was destruction and loss of human life" (Koponen, 2010: 24). Koponen (2010: 24) unfolds that,

> "The contemporary German sources abound with grim descriptions while African oral testimonies tell of brutalities of the askari of which even the mildest are revolting. On the German side the casualties were counted in hundreds: 15 Europeans, 71 askari, 316 auxiliaries. On the African side, tens, if not hundreds of thousands of people lost their lives, most of them civilians succumbing to famine deliberately unleashed by the German military after the operations. The rebels had been destroying crops of those who had declined to take maji but by far the worst casualties came from the systematic colonialist use of the scorched earth tactic."

There ensued a three-year famine that was incomparable to previous famines and consequently, many people denied their children as well as wives (*ibid.*: 24). Exact statistics on death toll due to Majimaji war are inaccurate and thus, several proponents, for example, Gwassa, who conducted his doctoral studies in the late 1960s, reported to be from 250,000 to 300,000 people died (*ibid.*: 24). Such human losses echoed generations ahead, for famine hurt human fertility as unveiled, for example, in results from a study in Ulanga, Morogoro region, that about 25 percent of the next generation remained unborn (*ibid.*: 24).

It is suggested that human losses were real and shocking but likely three points emerge (*ibid.*: 24). Firstly, it is difficult to know any exact numbers of death tolls and thus, it may be lower than the highest estimates imply; and secondly, human losses differed from place to place but it is acknowledged losses were mostly heavy "… in the Matumbi Hills and much of Ngindoland like in parts of Ungoni, Upangwa and Uvidunda" (*ibid.*: 24). Finally, "… from our present day vantage point, most of these areas must have more than fully recovered long ago in terms of population. After all, more than 100 years have now passed. The recovery has been uneven and taken many forms. There have been spirals both upwards and downwards" (*ibid.*: 24).

1.3.2   Internal changes

Majimaji war atrocities led to deep internal changes amongst Southern societies such that people migrated and settled in new places and thus, such population movements changed their leaders (Koponen, 2010: 25). Advanced reasons for such changes include the fact that many died on the battlefield and leaders who survived were executed as a whole and accordingly, leadership positions were accorded to a younger as well as differently inclined generation (*ibid.*: 25). It was most discernible among Wangoni ethnic group, "… whose top aristocracy, some 84 people, were hanged by the Germans in Songea in early 1906. Maji Maji basically destroyed the Ngoni military society and did much to level out the old distinction between aristocrats and subjects" (*ibid.*: 25). There were new appointments of chiefs from educated sons of the old ones and from subject Wandendeule people (*ibid.*: 25). Similar changes were noticeable elsewhere in the Majimaji war torn areas, for example, amongst Wangindo and Wamatumbi, entire clans died out (*ibid.*). "The execution of some 200 warriors wiped out the Vidunda leadership. Although some members of Mbeyela's family changed their names, the Germans distributed their territory to new leaders, some indigenous and others brought from outside" (*ibid.*: 25).

1.3.4   Changes from extractive to developmental colonialism

During the colonial government, there were policy changes and such major policy changes can be sketched back to Majimaji war (Koponen, 2010). Real policies after Majimaji war changed more gradually and in a highly contradictory way but seriously ensured to avoid a new uprising (*ibid.*).

Koponen (2010: 27) argues that Majimaji highly "… accelerated the shift from a basically extractive and largely trade-based colonial policy to a more developmental one - developmental in the modern sense of the word, combining intentional intervention with high-sounding purposes." In due regard, it was not a total shift because some elements of the developmental rule existed in the beginning, some elements of the extractive manner, particularly extensive use of obliged force in labour recruitment, remained (*ibid*.: 27). Thus, to a large extent, after the war, German colonialism went into the developmental manner much earlier than is generally renowned and later protectorate rulers after World War I, the British furthered such development (*ibid*.).

1.3.5 Development and neglect

Notably, Koponen (2010) holds that development in the colonial context means construction of infrastructure such as building of railways and roads, introduction of new crops together with cultivation methods, extension of missionary as well as colonial education and improvement of undeveloped health services. In the southern parts of Tanzania, evident devastation in the immediate outcome of Majimaji war seemed to provide little potential for development endeavors (*ibid*.).

After Majimaji war, colonialism forged ahead into a highly developmental mode but the southern areas of the country linked to Majimaji war were left outside development force and thus, they were largely neglected (*ibid*.). There was a plan to build a railway across the South from Kilwa to Lake Malawi, paralleling those built from the coast to Kigoma in the west along Lake Tanganyika shores and Arusha in the north of the country (*ibid*.). Nonetheless, the planned project was scrapped by the Germans (*ibid*.). Additionally, there was no systematic introduction of new cash crops "… after the ill-fated German cotton efforts…" (*ibid*.). Moreover, in the South, a great deal of education and health care services were left to hands of missionaries (*ibid*.).

Along places, Wangindo and other people lived in settlements of different sizes, where caravans of porters traversed along well-established trade routes and where the *maji* message was spread, the Selous Game Reserve was established (*ibid*.). The area's former residents were moved away and resettled thereby created a large piece of 'wilderness' (*ibid*.). Formation of the Selous was a long thought-out process and Majimaji war was one but decisive moment in it (*ibid*.).

1.4 Majimaji war genocide or not genocide?

Recall, Majimaji was a war of resistance and Germans "… referred to it as a rebellion, uprising or revolt but it is unrealistic to expect that a freedom movement should be called as such by those it opposed" (Gwassa, 1973: 38; Rushohora, 2015: 192). The idea or concept for that matter "… that local communities experienced 'genocide' at the hands of their white conquerors is not only dismissed, but openly…" was ridiculed by scholars (Rushohora, 2015: 192). Over a serious note is that colonial wars are not more often than not considered genocidal in intention, but they could, however, be genocidal in their effects (Rushohora, 2015: 192). It is repeatedly argued that during Majimaji war, the German military operations "… in the country cannot be called genocide because the murder of hundreds of thousands of the population in the colony was never the intentional goal of German warfare" (Rushohora, 2015: 193). It is argued further that Germans used pretexts that murders of a large part of local Tanzanian population were a grave accident (*ibid.*).

Notably, historians agree to the notion that people of southern Tanzania started Majimaji war who targeted the German authority (Gwassa, 1973: 8; Rushohora, 2015: 193) and accordingly, Majimaji war should be well thought-out destructive and genocidal. "However, the counter-charge of genocide on the part of Majimaji fighters cannot be sustained, as there is no incidence where genocide may occur as self-defence" (Rushohora, 2015: 193). As Rushohora (2015: 193) brings to attention, "The civilian population was systematically targeted: entire villages, fields and granaries were burnt and hunger was used as a weapon to bring the guerrilla fighters to their knees." For local people, an act referred to as a crime connotes resistance and it is called as patriotism or nationalism (*ibid.*).

Rushohora (2015: 193, 194) enlightens that,

> "Indeed, the German counter-insurgency campaign in southern Tanzania presents an extreme case of colonial violence which fulfils the criteria for genocide. There was intent to destroy the groups by killing, causing serious bodily or mental harm, and inflicting conditions calculated to bring about their physical destruction which are the features of genocide (Berat 1993:166). Article ii of the UN convention of 1948 defines genocide as any of the following acts committed with intent to destroy, in whole or in part, national, ethnic, racial or religious groups. These include killing members of a group; causing serious bodily or mental harm to members of the group; deliberately inflicting on the group conditions of life calculated to bring about its physical destruction in whole or in part; imposing measures intended

to prevent births within the group; and forcibly transferring children of the group to another group."

Important to note is that "The German troops used scorched earth policy (Larson, 2010: 110), gendercide (killing of women), genocidal hunger, extermination and mass killings, which were explicitly prohibited under the law of armed conflict which was applicable at the time and which the German imperial troops and their commanders chose to ignore" (Rushohora, 2015: 194). Rushohora (2015: 194) further informs that, "The German counter-insurgency campaign in southern Tanzania presents an extreme case of colonial violence which fulfils the criteria for genocide." Many scholars reported that German soldiers killed everyone in villages in the Majimaji war zone as well as raped pregnant women and thereafter, left them to die (for example, Gwassa and Iliffe, 1969: 23; Rushohora, 2015: 194). Additionally, in 1906, almost one hundred Wangoni elders were executed so as to eliminate the complete military and political elites (Rushohora, 2015: 194). Besides, Germans carried out military missions and killed traditional healers (Monson, 2010: 36-37).

German soldiers were involved in beheading African chiefs and kings as well as took their skulls to Germany on the pretext that they carried out treasonable offenses and some were hanged (LeGall, 2020). Such actions dehumanised heroes as well as heroines along with leaders and they were carried out through various processes with some remains of prominent leaders were regarded as deathly souvenirs of military achievements, while others were transported to Germany, they were further stored and studied by scientists (*ibid*.). Scientists measured and compared human remains from all over the world and such "… studies fuelled discourse on biological determinism and Social Darwinist assumptions on race. In the twentieth century, such theories were then politically instrumentalised for oppressive policies such as apartheid or the infamous Nuremberg laws" (*ibid*.: 9). It can be argued that such acts depict "…center of evidence of the colonial crime scene" (*ibid*.: 9).

Further war crimes involved beheading African leaders. The following African leaders were beheaded: Chief Songea Mbano of Songea in southern Tanzania was hanged, Mtwa (Chief) Mkwavinyika Mkwawa of Uhehe (now Iringa) Chiefdom (killed himself), Mkwawa's brother, Mpangile was hanged by Germans and his skull was taken to Germany, the skull of Mchagga anti-colonial leader Mangi (King) Meli of Kibosho in Kilimanjaro region was taken to Germany and Chief Nkunde (Mkunde) of Kibong'oto [(Kilimanjaro) *ibid*.]. Moreover, soldiers, doctors and researchers scrambled for getting skulls of indigenous leaders and were accumulated for ethnographic as well as physical anthropological data (*ibid*.: 9).

Furthermore, Majimaji atrocities involved other avenues that included neglect and thus, abandoned dead bodies of victims open/bare on landscapes. Majimaji war's severity resulted in non-burial of the dead because those who survived were too weak to dig graves owing to diseases as well as famine (Rushohora, 2015: 195). People's cadavers were left scattered on compounds to be scavenged by wild animals, for instance, lions and hyenas (Rushohora, 2015: 195). In due regard, denials of such important cultural rights like burial are absolutely genocide (Rushohora, 2015: 195).

In evaluation of Majimaji war, Bachmann's (2018: 170) submissions include important points to consider that,

> "There are strong indications pointing to a genocidal intent by some of the German commanders. In October 1905, Hauptmann von Wangenheim presented the scorched earth strategy as a means of ending partisan warfare by starvation: 'If the still remaining food is consumed and people's homes are destroyed and they lose the possibility to cultivate new fields because we conduct continuous raids, then they will have to give up their resistance.' Even some missionaries joined the call to fight the insurgents through starvation. Subsequently, the German troops destroyed fields and crops to the extent that they endangered their own food supplies. Von Götzen justified this hunger strategy by pointing to the alleged civilisatory inferiority of the enemy.25 The strategy was a success – the Maji-Maji uprising ended in a three year long mass starvation which devastated a large part of the southern part of the country. Young mothers were unable to feed their newborn babies, who perished in large numbers. Southern Usagara was entirely depopulated by 1906, in Ulanga, 25 percent of the women had become unfit to become pregnant. According to some estimations, one third of the pre-war population had died, with up to 300,000 casualties.26 The ecological consequences of the war triggered an expansion of the Tse-Tse infected parts of

the country, because the flies followed game which migrated into the depopulated."

As a result of all reported Majimaji war atrocities, there is the question, was Majimaji war genocide or not genocide? To contextualize the answer as to whether or not Majimaji war was genocide, the definition of genocide by the United Nations Genocide Convention is reproduced,

> "Genocide means any of the following acts committed with intent to destroy, in whole or in part, a national, ethnical, racial or religious group, as such: a. Killing members of the group; b. Causing serious bodily or mental harm to members of the group; c. Deliberately inflicting on the group conditions of life calculated to bring about its physical destruction in whole or in part; d. Imposing measures intended to prevent births within the group; e. Forcibly transferring children of the group to another group. The above definition was the result of a negotiating process and reflected the compromise reached among the UN member states" (*ibid*.: 9).

In further strengthening points for arguing for or not that Majimaji war was genocide, many actions point to the fact that it was genocide. The UN Genocide Convention informs it all. For example, the colonial system legalised forced labour, imprisonment, detention in chains and corporal punishment plainly known in English as whip and known by local people in Kiswahili as *kiboko* (Rushohora, 2019).

All together, such over-dependence on corporal punishment activated over 50 local wars of resistance against German colonialism was established between 1890 and 1908 and thus, they included Majimaji war conflicts from 1904 to 1908. In containing such eruptions of resistance, the German colonial rulers employed prisons for detention including execution of local warriors (*ibid*.). Accordingly, such acts form memories of German colonialism in Tanzania in associating prisons with confinement, pain, execution and organized option to violence furnish cultural genocide that were intentionally aimed to destroy lives including cultural identity of local communities (*ibid*.).

Accordingly, based on the United Nations Genocide Convention, the Majimaji war as reported in many research results was genocide. This stance can also be clearly imbued or permeated through Afrocentricity pertinently fitting in Asante's (2003: 268) rebuttal echoed by Watson (2015: 48) that,

"Afrocentrists have never opposed any racial group or supported any type of discrimination… true Afrocentrist[s] cannot support any racist doctrine but must insist on diversity of cultural positions and experiences without hierarchy – that is, without saying one is better than another or more advanced than the other…"

More importantly, caution is that the said interpretation that Majimaji war was genocide does not imply to get into unnecessary and unproductive debates. Based on Afrocentricity frame of reference, there is a safe position in furnishing comprehension of the African realities, in this case Majimaji war, a new visualization of the continent's past and present so as "… to liberate the minds of the ignorant or miseducated masses" (Rodrigue, 2020: 12).

1.5   Memory pertaining to Majimaji war

Heritage is concerning people collectively and as individuals as well as to their sense of inheritance from the past (Rushohora, 2015: 196). Heritage is human's legacy from the past, what people live with today and what people pass on to future generations (Rushohora, 2015: 196). Of special note is that violence is aggravated by strong emotions that render it both more obvious as well as memorable than most human actions (Rushohora, 2015: 196). Majimaji war is part of heritage of the colonial period and it holds a unique position in Tanzanian resistances against German colonialism (*ibid.*). Accordingly, it has memory, unique memory in the history of the country at diverse dimensions as it is shown in subsequent sub-sections.

For example, there is Majimaji war heritage landscape, which is embodied by a system of sites that were of significance during the war and they include "… refuges, settlement, battle sites and shrines" (Rushohora, 2015: 202). The refuge areas were more often normal areas as well as forests and refuge caves and they include the following: Nang'oma, Namaingo, Likorongomba, Nampombo, Mpatawa and Chingya, all in Umatumbi, as well as Chandamali in Songea (*ibid.*: 202). "Both refuges and settlements where people lived and produced required protection" (Rushohora, 2015: 202). Caves were enclosed with bushes with a lot of artificial entrances that were very significant for security (Rushohora, 2015: 202, 203). There are several caves that were prominent refuge places for Majimaji warriors and they include Namabengo, Liwale, Nyikamitwe and Mahenge (*ibid.*: 203).

Moreover, most landscape features supported warfare in different Majimaji communities. For example, the Matumbi hills were advantageous for seeing enemies from far away and thus, "... made it easier to prepare for the attack; Lukuledi River provided an escarpment suitable for hideout and attack; the Lupagaro Mountains and Ruhira River in Ungoni provided refuge for the warriors. In the whole course of the war, rituals played an important part" (*ibid.*: 204).

Diviners and their shrines used to communicate with ancestors accordingly furnish another significant heritage of the landscape and most shrines were community shrines (*ibid.*: 204). However, shrines were destroyed before and after the war, for example, Ng'anda ya Nyasele at Namakinga in Ungoni "... was burnt by the missionary before the Majimaji war" (*ibid.*: 204). The shrine "... was the main spiritual shrine of the Ngoni Njelu kingdom where the chief (nkosi) revered his ancestors, held rain rituals and made sacrifices to ensure social harmony and the soil's fertility (Rushohora, 2015: 204). Ritual specialists are associated with specific locations where they communicated with ancestral spirits (Monson, 2010:4). The African healing place is considered as a sanctuary (Monson, 2010: 44).

Additionally, other landscapes include crossroads that are also associated with rituals (Sunseri, 1997: 13; Rushohora, 204). Numerous

> "... attacks on three fronts by the Majimaji warriors were directed at the crossroads, for example, the attack on Somanga and Liwale boma (Gwassa 1969). While this is regarded as a military technique, the attack may also have been facilitated by the rituals that the communities enacted at the crossroads. The Maji medicine was also obtained from a "T-junction"–a confluence or meeting point of rivers Namang'ondo and Ngarambe. Thus, the crossroads attack was probably a part of the Majimaji war ritual" (Rushohora, 2015: 204).

Notably, landscape carried bodies of the dead from the war and they were not interred in formal graves (*ibid.*). Accordingly, landscapes of communities involved in the war are important as heritage landscapes and commemoration of war heritage landscape presents an important "... heritage memorial which does not exclude episodes which led to the war, contributed to the cause of the war or mark the aftermath of the war" (*ibid.*: 204). A conversion of battlefields to heritage places is often a process whereby they become memorialized in some manner to mark them as significant (Rushohora, 2015: 204).

Furthermore, associations of a name with an event serve to safeguard the memory in the landscape (*ibid.*: 205). There are additional landscape heritages that furnished water, for example, at convergence of Namang'ondo and Ngarambe Rivers that were sources of *maji*, Kinjekitile's house and a natural spring associated with Kinjekitile's rituals (*ibid.*: 205).

1.6   Repatriation and reparation

There are two important aspects related to Majimaji communities, repatriation and reparation (Rushohora, 2015: 205). Even though German militants did not admit having committed to be-heading "… and preservation of skulls as trophies during the Majimaji war, their *askari* (soldier/police) apparently mutilated enemy corpses and cut off the genitalia of the dead warriors to prove that they had killed combatants" (Rushohora, 2015: 205). Also, some leaders' skulls, for example, Mkwawa were beheaded and his skull was taken to Germany. However, it was repatriated to Tanzania and a site museum at Kalenga, in Iringa municipality outskirts was established. It houses Chief Mkwawa's skull, his belonging and other artifacts. Other African leaders who were beheaded include the following: Chief Songea Mbano of Songea in southern Tanzania was hanged, the head of Mkwawa's brother, Mpangile was hanged by Germans and his skull was taken to Germany, the skull of Mchagga anti-colonial leader Mangi (King) Meli of Kibosho in Kilimanjaro region was taken to Germany, and Chief Nkunde (Mkunde) of Kibong'oto [(Kilimanjaro) LeGall, 2020].

Disposal of body parts is uncertain and has remained a suffering in Majimaji war torn communities. It is reported that Nduna (Chief) Songea Mbano's family members, "… the War General in Ungoni," are convinced that the head of their grandfather was not buried with his body. According to them, the head was taken by the Germans as a trophy. Written sources are mute on whether the head of Chief Songea was buried with his body or taken as the family claims.

Sometimes repatriation is a symbol of autonomy (Nesper 2002: 187). Repatriation serves as a catalyst for processes of public and civic mourning, without which people living in societies torn by ethnic conflict and crimes against humanity may be unable to find healing (Pikirayi 2007: 311; Rushohora, 2015: 205).

In another vein, there is a mass grave at Majimaji Memorial Museum in Songea but it does not represent the southern Tanzanian burial site

(Rushohora, 2015: 206). Communities of Songea want to have the graves of their forefathers at their families' burial grounds but the mass grave is a symbol of all who died during Majimaji war (*ibid.*: 206). Estimates for those buried at the said mass grave account for 100 or more "… bodies of warriors who were hanged after summary execution by Major Johannes on three dates: 27 February, 20 March and 12 April 1906" (*ibid.*: 206). It was reported that all the way through Majimaji communities, people demand reparation (*ibid.*: 206). In due regard, based on Afrocentricity paradigmatic stance, repatriation is necessary because it helps to observe aspects enlightened in Afrocentricity that,

> "Afrocentrists have never opposed any racial group or supported any type of discrimination… true Afrocentrist[s] cannot support any racist doctrine but must insist on diversity of cultural positions and experiences without hierarchy – that is, without saying one is better than another or more advanced than the other……."

1.7 Women and heroines in the Majimaji war

Rushohora (2015: 207) notes that very little attention was devoted to Majimaji war heroines. Even though Nkomanile, who was one of sub-chiefs in Ungoni, is widely discussed, the discussion is limited to initiation of recruits into the war in the south western regions through Omari Kinjala (Iliffe, 1967: 173; Rushohora, 2015: 209). Such stance leaves a gap pertaining to other aspects of Nkomanile "… including Kitanda as a gendered site, the burial of this female heroine with other males in the mass grave, and an opposition to the common emphasis on both physical and emotional differences between men and women, associating men with strength, aggression and violence and women with their opposites" (Rushohora, 2015: 205). Kitanda was the area where the female sub-chief Nkomanile ruled and it was the gate through which the magic water from Kinjekitile passed to Wangoni and later Upangwa as well as Ubena who too participated in Majimaji war (*ibid.*: 205). The only female sub-chief who participated in Majimaji war, Nkomanile was buried in a mass grave and she is the only woman who was sentenced to death by the Germans (*ibid.*).

Using Afrocentricity as a pertinent analytical lens and thus, position germane scholastic undertakings that have to unravel many aspects in an

African-centred perspective, studies must be carried out on Nkomanile as an agent of the war and should be broadened to the extent of pinpointing where and how gender is included in material discourse as well as investigate outcomes of its presence (see also, Rushohora, 2015: 205). "Landscape can be deduced as one of the factors in the delineation of Kitanda as the route to Ungoni. Kitanda was the beginning of the Ngoni Mchope chiefdom in the proximity of the Ungindo. Nkomanile was renowned for having ruled Kitanda with generosity and intelligent leadership (Mapunda, 2010: 228). Nkomanile was convinced of the power of *maji* and passed the information to her superiors who also subscribed to the cause of war and, of course, people of southern Tanzania hated colonialism (Rushohora, 2015: 201, 210).

Nkomanile participated in Majimaji war, she was persecuted and sentenced to death like other leaders as well as warriors of the Ungoni (*ibid.*: 210). But others were not persecuted , for example, Namabengo is another woman with a leadership position but her stance in begging for clemency did not lead to her being persecuted by Germans (*ibid.*). She persuaded the Germans that she did not join the war though it was probably not true and thus, the Germans spared her life (*ibid.*).

Moreover, all the way through the Majimaji war, women were involved in different contexts (*ibid.*: 211). Rushohora's work (2015: 211, 212) provides that,

> "According to the local informant Mrs. Thalitha Upunda, among the Matumbi of Nandete, Jumbe Mtemangani (junior German local representative) sent a letter to his superior at Kibata through his wife Namchanjama. This was after all his immediate officers, including Mtemangani himself refused to take the letter in fear of the reaction. Namchanjama was to report to the Akida (senior German local representative) Seif bin Amri at Kibata German administrative offices. Namchanjama was willing to take the letter and delivered the message. She was killed at Imbiliya hill upon her return to Nandete in a fierce battle between the German representatives at Kibata and Matumbi warriors. Namchanjama was among the first people who died in the Majimaji war."

Notably, women's participation and role in Majimaji war were diverse and for that matter, "… women are as much a factor as armies, formal or informal" (Rushohora, 2015: 212). For instance, *maji*, the war medicine, was managed by women who were considerable as well as included elements in ritual activities and in war (Monson, 2010: 37). Whereas men used war medicines to guarantee accuracy of firearms, women took medicines to reinforce them against hardship of flight into woodland hiding places and preserve them from capture by enemies (Rushohora, 2015: 212). Moreover, women were used as spies (Rushohora, 2015: 212). In due regard, colonial troops detained women as hostages so as "… to establish whether they were Majimaji supporters or loyalists" (*ibid.*: 212). The technique intended to force surrender by preventing supplies reaching the warrior bands but acknowledged the important role women played during the warfare (Schmidt, 2010: 206-207).

1.8 Majimaji heritage Resources

The Majimaji war heritage is of the colonial era and accordingly, the war has a distinctive position in Tanzanian resistances against German colonialism (Rushohora, 2015). Majimaji heritage is in form of artifacts and structures (*ibid.*). In Songea municipality, there is a grave yard of several Majimaji warriors including remains of Chief Songea. Besides, the place for hanging is preserved as well as conserved and all of such heritages compose the Majimaji War Memorial. Additionally, in February of every year, the government, through the Ministry of Natural Resources and Ruvuma Region authority, carry out Majimaji War commemorative ceremonies in Songea at the Majimaji War Memorial Museum, branch of the National Museums of Tanzania whereby many people of all categories are involved at diverse capacities.

1.8.1 Majimaji heritage sites

Based on nature of Majimaji war, there are varied Majimaji war heritage sites that include the German boma or administration headquarters, the missionary centres that were attacked in the war and the constructed Majimaji Memorial Museum at Songea (Rushohora, 2015: 196). After the war, German administration offices, particularly the court and prisons were used to detain war prisoners, persecute as well as hang them (*ibid.*: 196). Besides, the German administration areas were graves of some of the Majimaji warriors. Accordingly, some structures constructed by Germans linked to Majimaji war include the following: Kilwa, Liwale, Barikiwa, Lindi, Songea, Mahenge, Muhoro and Utete (Rushohora, 2015: 197).

Another Majimaji war heritage category includes missionary centres such that they were targets by the local communities because they considered them accomplices of German administrators (Rushohora, 2015: 197). For example, based on such claims, the church of Kigonsera was burnt because Wangoni feared from its use as a German military post (Rushohora, 2015: 197). Besides, some missionaries were killed and churches were burnt during the Majimaji war (Rushohora, 2015: 197). They include the following places that were burnt due to Majimaji war: Peramiho, Lukuledi and Nyangao including a missionary school at Mititimo. Thus, all such places in southern Tanzania that were under Majimaji war are part of the war heritage (*ibid.*: 198).

Furthermore, the Majimaji War Memorial Museum in Songea is another war heritage including Majimaji war mass grave yard (*ibid.*: 198). Its importance as a war heritage is due to the fact that the museum represents the only known Majimaji war grave yard where warriors as well as leaders of Ungoni were buried during Majimaji war (*ibid.*: 198). "To the communities, the museum is not only a memorial but also a shrine" (*ibid.*: 198).

1.8.2 Majimaji heritage landscapes

The landscape into which Majimaji war happened in its various forms or dimensions and its outcomes forms part known as Majimaji heritage landscape. Thus, landscapes of communities that were involved in Majimaji warfare make meaningful as heritage landscapes (Rushohora, 2015: 205). Of further consideration is that,

> "… Majimaji was a conflict of environmental control that came with German colonialism (Sunseri, 2010: 119); thus, some of the Majimaji heritage is in the form of landscape. To Garden (2008: 271), all heritage sites are landscapes. However, what is construed here as the Majimaji heritage landscape is both a physical and a symbolic legacy of events that took place over the landscape and the meaning inherited from generation to generation" (Rushohora, 2015: 201).

In due regard, Majimaji heritage landscape encompasses colonial projects, for example, plantations, industry, trade, village settlements, refuges, shrines, burials and toponymic heritage (*ibid.*: 201, 202). Recall, in the country, colonialists established agriculture, trade and industries to exploit raw materials but colonial projects were sources of many resistances in Africa. People's participation to Majimaji war differed from one region to another region (Sunseri, 2010: 141; Rushohora, 2015: 202). It is reported that Nandete cotton plantation is the site of symbolic origin of Majimaji war because it is the place where Majimaji war was declared (Rushohora, 2015: 202). Moreover, in 1903 in Liwale, trade in wild rubber was banned and there was replacement of rubber as well as cotton plantations and such measures were drives for Majimaji war (Larson, 2010:100). There are networks of Majimaji war heritage sites that encompass refuges, settlement, battle sites including shrines and refuge areas that were mostly caves as well as forests (Rushohora, 2015: 202). The refuge caves as Majimaji heritage landscapes include the following: Nang'oma, Namaingo, Likorongomba, Nampombo, Mpatawa and Chingya, all in Umatumbi, and Chandamali in Songea (*ibid.*: 202).

Additionally, there are several Majimaji heritage war sites where Majimaji warriors encountered Germans face-to-face and they include Namabengo, Liwale, Nyikamitwe and Mahenge (*ibid.*: 203). Also, hilly or mountainous areas were important for Majimaji warriors as hideout places or as places that gave proper vision to note their enemies for afar, for instance, "… the Matumbi hills gave the advantage of seeing the enemies from afar and therefore made it easier to prepare for the attack; the Lukuledi River provided an escarpment suitable for hideout and attack; the Lupagaro Mountains and Ruhira River in Ungoni provided refuge for the warriors" (*ibid.*: 203).

Besides, "The ritualists and their shrines used to communicate with the ancestors mark another important heritage of the landscape. Most of these shrines were community shrines. Shrines were destroyed before and after the war. Ng'anda ya Nyasele at Namakinga in Ungoni, for example, was burnt by the missionary before the Majimaji war" (*ibid.*: 203). The place "… was the main spiritual shrine of the Ngoni Njelu kingdom where the chief (nkosi) revered his ancestors, held rain rituals, and made sacrifices to ensure social harmony and the soil's fertility" (Rushohora, 2015: 203). Thus, shrines used by people for Majimaji war are heritage landscape sites.

Moreover, crossroads are associated too with rituals (Rushohora, 2015: 203) and for the case of Majimaji war, "… many attacks were directed at the crossroads, for example, the attack on Somanga and Liwale boma" (Gwassa, 1969). It is reported that, "… Maji medicine was also obtained from a "T-junction" – a confluence or meeting point of rivers Namang'ondo and Ngarambe" (Rushohora, 2015: 204). Of special note is that "… the landscape also carries bodies of all who died in the war and were not buried in any formal grave. Most descendants of the victims, whether those killed in combat or by starvation and related causes, were left without a site to revere their ancestors (Rushohora, 2015: 204).

1.9 Concluding Remarks

Recall, this chapter under the theme, "In memory of genocide against members of Majimaji Movement in Tanzania from 1905 to 1907" provides a review of other scholars' works in various disciplines including History, Literature, Historical Archaeology and Ethnoarchaeology. The review is based on advocates' research endeavours at various dimensions that include historical data sets, principally from unpublished historical sources (notably, archival materials, oral accounts and published data sets. Different aspects to memorise, discuss, functionalise or to deny and minimise genocide against members of the Majimaji Movement are furnished.

As already noted, this chapter is presented because there are many interpretations about Majimaji war based on a fair amount of research endeavours but the facts seem to provide room for many contentious questions or polarisation. For example, the manner the revolts were called in the beginning by German colonists as Majimaji rebellion, while during struggles for the country's independence and after independence, the battle was called and is still called, Majimaji war. Recall, water in Kiswahili is known as *maji* and hence, the said independence struggles were called Majimaji war. Moreover, the mayhem and thus, consequences of the war are variously interpreted with some calling genocide to both Africans and Germans, while others refrain from mentioning the said inhuman actions.

Generally, causes of Majimaji war include the following: forced cotton cultivation as well as rubber extraction; heavy taxation; enforced ordinances as well as rules for people's abolishment of activities in exploiting natural resources and compulsory labour together with harassment in road construction.

In 1905, Majimaji war erupted with varying intensity across most parts of the territory and Lindi as well as Kilwa districts were areas where the uprising first broke out in the country. Majimaji war spread to other parts of the country organised as well as spearheaded by both men and women warriors from about 20 different ethnic groups that included Wamatumbi, Wangindo, Wapogoro, Wamwera, Wayao and Wangoni, just to mention a few. The war ended in 1907. Majimaji war had the following consequences: devastation and depopulation; internal changes; changes from extractive to developmental colonialism; and development as well as neglect.

Devastation and depopulation can be observable whereby Majimaji war led to destruction and loss of human life. Exact statistics on death toll due to Majimaji are inaccurate and several advocates, for example, reported that from 250,000 to 300,000 people died. Additionally, Majimaji war atrocities led to deep internal changes amongst Southern societies such that people migrated and settled in new places and thus, such population movements changed their leaders.

During the colonial government, there were policy changes and major policy changes can be sketched back to Majimaji war. Accordingly, real policies after Majimaji war changed more gradually and in a highly contradictory way but seriously ensured to avoid a new uprising or revolt.

In the southern parts of Tanzania, evident **devastation** in the immediate outcome of Majimaji seemed to provide little potential for development endeavours. After Majimaji war, colonialism forged ahead into a highly developmental mode but the southern areas of the country linked to Majimaji war were left outside development force and thus, they were largely neglected. For instance, there was a plan to build a railway across the South from Kilwa to Lake Malawi, paralleling those built from the coast to Kigoma in the west along Lake Tanganyika shores and Arusha in the north of the country but the planned project was scrapped by the Germans.

Memory pertaining to Majimaji war is evident through heritage. Of special note is that violence is aggravated by strong emotions that render it both more obvious as well as memorable than most human actions (Rushohora, 2015: 196). Majimaji war is part of heritage of the colonial period and it holds a unique position in Tanzanian resistances against German colonialism (*ibid.*). Accordingly, it has memory, unique memory in the history of the country at diverse dimensions – landscapes including graves, shrines and crossroads (mainly associated with rituals that were also important for Majimaji war).

There are two important aspects related to Majimaji communities, **repatriation and reparation** (Rushohora, 2015: 205). Even though German militants did not admit having committed to be-heading but testimony is accorded, for example, "…preservation of skulls as trophies during the Majimaji war, their *askari* (soldier/police) apparently mutilated enemy corpses and cut off the genitalia of the dead warriors to prove that they had killed combatants." Moreover, there is a mass grave at the Majimaji Memorial Museum in Songea but it does not represent the entire southern Tanzanian burial sites (*ibid.*: 206). Songea communities want to have graves of their forefathers at their families' burial grounds but the mass grave is a symbol of all who died during Majimaji war (*ibid*). Advocates reported that all the way through Majimaji communities, people demand reparation (*ibid.*: 206). In due regard, based on Afrocentricity paradigmatic stance, repatriation is necessary because it helps to observe aspects as enlightened that,

> "Afrocentrists have never opposed any racial group or supported any type of discrimination… true Afrocentrist[s] cannot support any racist doctrine but must insist on diversity of cultural positions and experiences without hierarchy – that is, without saying one is better than another or more advanced than the other…."

Women and heroines in the Majimaji war: Women were involved in Majimaji war at varying dimensions or capacities. For instance, Rushohora (2015: 207) notes that very little attention was devoted to Majimaji war heroines and although Nkomanile, who was one of sub-chiefs in Ungoni, is widely discussed but the discussion is limited to initiation of recruits into the war in the south western regions. Women's participation and role in Majimaji war were diverse and "… women are as much a factor as armies, formal or informal" (Rushohora, 2015: 212). Furthermore, *maji*, the war medicine, was managed by women who were considerable as well as included elements in ritual activities and in war (Monson, 2010: 37). Whereas men used war medicines to guarantee accuracy of firearms, women took medicines to reinforce them against hardship of flight into woodland hiding places and preserve them from capture by enemies (Rushohora, 2015: 212). Moreover, women were used as spies (Rushohora, 2015: 212). Therefore, colonial troops detained women as hostages so as "… to establish whether they were Majimaji supporters or loyalists" (*ibid.*: 212). This technique intended to force surrender by preventing supplies in reaching the warrior groups but also acknowledged the important role women played during the warfare (*ibid.*).

Majimaji heritage resources: The Majimaji war heritage is of the colonial era and accordingly, the war has a distinctive position in Tanzanian resistances against German colonialism (Rushohora, 2015). Majimaji heritage is in form of artifacts and structures (*ibid.*). In Songea municipality, there is a grave yard of several Majimaji warriors including remains of Chief Songea. Besides, the place for hanging is preserved as well as conserved and all of such heritages compose the Majimaji War Memorial. Additionally, in February of every year, the government, through the Ministry of Natural Resources and Ruvuma Region authority, carries out Majimaji War commemorative ceremonies in Songea at the Majimaji War Memorial Museum, branch of the National Museums of Tanzania whereby many people of all categories are involved at diverse capacities.

Was Majimaji war genocide or not genocide? This is the most important aspect delved in this chapter by providing a positive decipherment of the said war and its consequences, the atrocities. As a result of all reported Majimaji war atrocities, there is the question, was Majimaji war **genocide or not genocide?** A succinct response as to whether or not Majimaji war was genocide is in research results and the definition of genocide by the United Nations Genocide Convention that,

> "Genocide means any of the following acts committed with intent to destroy, in whole or in part, a national, ethnical, racial or religious group, as such: a. Killing members of the group; b. Causing serious bodily or mental harm to members of the group; c. Deliberately inflicting on the group conditions of life calculated to bring about its physical destruction in whole or in part; d. Imposing measures intended to prevent births within the group; e. Forcibly transferring children of the group to another group. The above definition was the result of a negotiating process and reflected the compromise reached among the UN member states" (Bachmann, 2018: 9).

In further strengthening points for arguing for or not that Majimaji war was genocide, many actions point to the fact that it was genocide. The UN Genocide Convention informs it all. For example, the colonial system legalised forced labour, imprisonment, detention in chains and corporal punishment plainly known in English as whip and known by local people in Kiswahili as *kiboko* (Rushohora, 2019). In curbing such eruptions of resistance, the German colonial rulers employed prisons for detention including execution of local warriors (*ibid.*). As a result, such acts form memories of German colonialism in Tanzania in associating prisons with confinement, pain, execution and organized option to violence, which furnish cultural genocide that were intentionally meant to destroy lives including cultural identity of local communities (*ibid.*).

Accordingly, based on the United Nations Genocide Convention, the Majimaji war as reported in many research results was genocide. This stance can also be clearly permeated through Afrocentricity pertinently fitting in Asante's (2003: 268) rebuttal echoed by Watson (2015: 48) that, "Afrocentrists have never opposed any racial group or supported any type of discrimination… true Afrocentrist[s] cannot support any racist doctrine but must insist on diversity of cultural positions and experiences without hierarchy – that is, without saying one is better than another or more advanced than the other…" Therefore, Majimaji war was genocide based on Afrocentricity frame of reference and accordingly, there is a safe position in furnishing comprehension of the African realities, in this case Majimaji war, a new visualization of the continent's past and present so as "… to liberate the minds of the ignorant or miseducated masses" (Rodrigue, 2020: 12).

References

Anderson, Reynaldo (2012). "MolefI Kete Asante: The Afrocentric Idea and the cultural turn in intercultural communication studies." *International Journal of Intercultural Relations*. 36, (6): 760-769. https://doi.org/10.1016/j.ijintrel.2012.08.005 Get rights and content.

Asante, M. K. (2007). *An Afrocentric Manifesto: Toward an African Renaissance*. Cambridge: Polity Press.

Asante, M. K. (1987). *The Afrocentric idea*. Philadelphia, PA: Temple University Press.

Bachmann, Klaus (2018). Genocidal Empires: German Colonialism in Africa and the Third Reich. Eds. by Anna Wolff-Powęska & Piotr Forecki. Berlin: Peter Lang.

Bangura, Abdul Karim (2012). "From Diop to Asante: Conceptualizing and Contextualizing the Afrocentric Paradigm." The Journal of Pan African Studies. 5(1): 103 – 125.

Becker, F. (2004). "Traders, Big Men and Prophets: Political Continuity and Crisis in the Maji Maji Rebellion in Southeast Tanzania." *The Journal of African History*. 45(1): 1-22.

De Juan, A. (2016). "Extraction and Violent Resistance in the Early Phases of State Building: Quantitative Evidence From the 'Maji Maji' Rebellion, 1905-1907." *Comparative political studies* 49(3): 291-323. https://doi.org/10.1177/0010414015617962.

Ebner, E. (2009). *The History of the Wangoni*. Peramiho and Ndanda: Benedictine Publication.

Flemming, Tracy Keith (2017). "Africology: An Introductory Descriptive Review of Disciplinary Ancestry." Africology: The Journal of Pan African Studies. 11(1): 319 - 388

Gregory, Athanasy (2020). "The Role of Women in Maji Maji War from 1905 to 1907 in Matumbiland, Ngindo and Ngoniland War Zones, Tanzania." East African Journal of Education and Social Sciences. 1(3): 52-59. DOI: https://doi.org/10.46606/eajess2020v01i03.0042 URL: http://eajess.ac.tz

Greiner, Andreas (2022). "Colonial Schemes and African Realities: Vernacular Infrastructure and the Limits of Road Building in German East Africa." The Journal of African History 63(3): 328–347 doi:10.1017/S0021853722000500

Gwassa, G. C. K. (2005). *The Outbreak and Development of the Maji Maji War 1905–1907*. Berlin: InterCultura-Missions-und Kulturgeschichtliche Forschungen.

Gwassa, G.C.K. (1973). "The Outbreak and Development of the Maji Maji War, 1905-1907." Ph.D. Thesis, University of Dar es Salaam.

Gwassa, G. C. K. (1969). "African Methods of Warfare during Maji Maji War 1905–1907." *Social Science Council of the University of East Africa* 1: 256–72.

Iliffe, J. (1969). "Tanzania Under German and British Rule." in Zamani: A Survey of East African History, ed. B. A. Ogot and J. A. Kieran, pp. 2 90-301. Nairobi: East African Publishing House.

Khokholkova, Nadezhda (2016). "Afrocentricity: The Evolution of the Theory in the Context of American History." Social Evolution & History 15(1): 111–125.

Koponen, J. (2010). "Maji Maji in the Making of the South." *Tanzania Zamani: A Journal of History Research and Writing*. 7(1): 1-58. http://hdl.handle.net/10138/252452

Larson, L. (2010). "The Ngindo: Exploring the Center of the Maji Maji Rebellion," in Giblin, J., & Monson, J. (Eds) *Maji Maji Lifting the Frog of War*. pp 71-114. Leiden, Boston: Brill. DOI: https://doi.org/10.1163/ej.9789004183421.i-325.18

Lawi, Y. 2009. "Pros and Cons of Patriotism in the Teaching of the Maji Maji War in Tanzania Schools." *Journal of Historical Association of Tanzania* 6(2):66-90.

LeGall, Yann (2020). "Songea Mbano and the 'halfway dead' of the Majimaji War (1905–7) in memory and theatre." *Human Remains and Violence.* 6(2): 4–22. http://dx.doi.org/10.7227/HRV.6.2.

Mapunda, B. B. (2010). "Re-examining the Maji Maji War in Ungoni with a Blend of Archaeology and Oral History." In eds. J. Giblin and J. Manson, *Maji Maji: Lifting the Fog of War*. pp. 220-238. Leiden, Boston: Brill.

Monson, J. (2010). War of Words: The narrative efficacy of medicine in the Maji Maji War. In eds. Giblin, J. and Monson, J. *Maji Maji Lifting the Fog of War. Pp. 33 – 69*. Leiden, Boston: Brill.

Mwaifuge, Eliah. S. (2014). "German Colonialism, Memory and Ebrahim Hussein's Kinjeketile." *Research on Humanities and Social Sciences.* 4(28): 37 – 48.

Odello, Marco and Piotr Łubiński, Piotr eds. (2020). *The Concept of Genocide in International Criminal Law*. New York: Rotledge

Rodrigue, Taling Tene (2020). "Sinafricology: A Paradigm Shift from African Studies to Chinese Africology/Africanology in Chinese Academia." *Journal of Education and Practice*. 11(9): 11-24.

Rushohora, Nancy, A. (2019). "Graves, Houses of Pain and Execution: Memories of the German Prisons after the Majimaji War in Tanzania (1904–1908)." *The Journal of Imperial and Commonwealth History*. 47(2): 275 - 299. DOI: 10.1080/03086534.2019.1605697

Rushohora, N.A., (2017). "Theorising the Majimaji – Landscape, Memory and Agency." *Journal of African Cultural Heritage Studies*. 1(1): 19–31. DOI: http://doi.org/10.22599/jachs.11.

Rushohora, Nancy Alexander (2015). "An Archaeological Identity of the Majimaji: Towards an Historical Archaeology of Resistance to German Colonisation in Southern Tanzania." PhD Thesis, University of Pretoria

Rushohora, Nancy. A. & Kurmman. E. (2017). "Looking at Majimaji! A Plea for Historical Photographs in Tanzania." *African Studies*. 77(1): 87-104, DOI: 10.1080/00020184.2017.1395584.

Rushohora, Nancy and Silayo, Valence (2019). "Cults, Crosses, and Crescents: Religion and Healing from Colonial Violence in Tanzania." Religions 10(9): 519. Doi:10.3390/rel10090519.

Shiraz, D. (1984). "Maji Maji: The Tanzanian People's War of National Liberation against German Colonialism, 1904-1907." Sauti ya Kamukunji, 3(1): 10–12.

Shockley, K.G., & Frederick, R.M. (2010). "Constructs and dimensions of Afrocentric Education." Journal of Black Studies, 40(6): 1212-1233.

Sunseri, T. (2010). "The War of the Hunters: Maji Maji and the Decline of the Ivory Trade." in Maji Maji Lifting the Fog of War, ed. J. Giblin and J. Monson, pp. 117-148. Brill, Boston

Watson, Marcia J. (2015). "Afrocentricity for All: A Case Study Examining the SelfHealing Power of Alternative Curricula as a Mediating Tool of Inclusion." A PhD dissertation in Curriculum and Instruction, University of North Carolina at Charlotte.

CHAPTER TWO

CULTURAL DIVERSITY IN TANZANIA AND GERMANY

By Dr. Sakina Faru

2.0 Introduction

This chapter presents a scholarly review on the theme, "Cultural Diversity in Tanzania and Germany." The chapter, based on socio-cultural dimensions, starts with definitions of key terms and concepts before presentation of the main text. Cultural diversity aspects, for example, gender diversity including interactions, are highlighted in the presentation. For good grasp, this chapter is organized through the following periods or eras experienced by Tanzania: interactions before colonialism, interactions during; colonialism interactions post-independence to date; and concluding remarks.

2.1 Definition of key terms and concepts

The term culture was succinctly defined by a British Anthropologist, Sir Edward Burnett Tylor in his book, "Primitive Culture" published in 1871. According to Tylor (Kottak, 2004: 344, 345), "Culture... is that complex whole, which includes knowledge, belief, art, morals, law, custom and any other capabilities and habits acquired by man as a member of society."

The Oxford English Dictionary defines diversity as "... the practice or quality of including or involving people from a range of different social and ethnic backgrounds and of different genders, social orientations, and so forth."

Cultural diversity usually "... refers to a reality of coexistence of diverse knowledge, beliefs, arts, morals, laws, customs, religions, languages, abilities and disabilities, genders, ethnicities, races, nationalities, sexual orientations, etc., of human beings" (Lin, 2019: 1). Notably, the United Nations has a Universal Declaration on Cultural Diversity for people around the world to observe such important cultural aspects.

2.2   Interactions before colonialism

In Tanzania, like anywhere around the world and the rest of Africa, the areas were inhabited by local people. They endured their livelihoods in socio-economic aspects with themselves and other people away from their local areas within the country including other areas in Africa whereby they were involved in trades of various kinds.

Based on ethnicity, most communities in pre-colonial times were governed by leadership styles that facilitated their cultural interactions within their communities and neighbourhood communities. Some ethnic groups were led by highly centralized political systems through chiefdoms. For example, in southern highlands of Tanzania, there was Chief Mtwa Mkwawa of Uhehe; in central Tanzania, Chief Mirambo of Tabora; in northern Tanzania, Mangi (Chief) Meli of Moshi in Kilimajaro and Nduna (Chief) Songea of Ungoni in southern Tanzania. On the other hand, some communities, particularly in Lindi as well as Mtwara in south-eastern Tanzania, involved ethnic groups that governed themselves through clan leadership system.

In another vein, two dominant life ways persisted and still persist that included, in great majority, patrilineal system, especially in southern highlands, central Tanzania and Lake Victoria areas, while matrilineal system was and still is, abound in coastal areas, particularly in Pwani, Lindi, Mtwara and Morogoro regions, to mention a few. Patrilineal system is a form of family in which authority is centred on the husband or father. In patrilineal families, the head of the family is a male and authority is vested in him. Additionally, in patrilineal communities, land is inherited through the male lineage and property passes directly to sons. Women have secondary rights because they can have access to it through their husbands and sons.

On the other hand, matrilineal society (for instance, Wamakonde, Wamakua and Wayao in south-eastern Tanzania) is a group adhering to a kinship system in which ancestral descent is traced through maternal instead of paternal lines. Accordingly, different from patrilineal societies, matrilineal societies have been thriving with women at the top for centuries and in such communities, women oversee everything from politics, economics and the broad social structure.

Uniform binding cultural life ways were practised by all communities, whether patrilineal or matrilineal. Their communications were through their vernacular languages within their ethnic groups that were predominantly Bantu. Additionally, social aspects including marriages were confined within ethnicity that included bride wealth, polygamy and few practiced monogamy.

Moreover, all local people in pre-colonial times carried out their livelihoods through farming for subsistence, while others were solely pastoralists (for example, Wamaasai, Wadatoga, Wamang'ati), some practiced agro-pastoralism (for instance, Wagogo, Wasukuma, Wanyamwezi as well as many others) and very few, for example, Wasandawe and Wahadzabe, were and still are, hunter gatherers. The hunter-gather societies and pastoralists' leadership style is in age sets and thus, did not have chiefdoms.

Furthermore, most communities along the coast of the Indian Ocean had long standing cultural connections that later paved the way for building closeness to trans-oceanic economic as well as cultural links (Unangst, 2015). In the eighth century, such people who lived along the East African coast were first heavily involved in international trading networks because Indian and Arabian slavers including merchants began travelling beyond in the hinterland on their trading expeditions (*ibid.*). By the twelfth century, people of the coast, who commenced calling themselves Swahili, after the Arabic word for coast, were converted to Islam even though they integrated it with their previous religious practices thereby formed their own combined type of Islam (*ibid.*). Such cultural diversity or cultural blend between African Bantu groups and foreigners, particularly Arabs blended a unique cultural tradition known as Swahili culture (Rushohora, 2015: 175). Accordingly, Swahili culture had its origins evident through pottery tradition attributed to the Swahili dating from thirteenth to nineteenth century (*ibid.*).

Additionally, people distinguished themselves from those inland based on the Kiswahili concept they called themselves *wastarabu*, a kind of Arabness, as a symbol of superiority of Islamic culture over those who were non-Islamic (*ibid.*). They displayed their cultural aspects that connected them to Arabia, particularly Islam and Kiswahili language (*ibid.*). In fact, by that time, to ease language of communication, Kiswahili was used by traders, explorers, missionaries and administrative personnel (Wójtowicz, 2022). The coastal society, or as they were known as Swahili society, depended on the following three concepts: *ustaarabu*, meaning "long standing and wise tradition;" *utamaduni*, meaning "urbanity or belonging to a town;" and *ushenzi*, meaning "barbarism" (Unangst, 2015). Notably, Islam distinguished a person of coastal society from those in hinterland that involved links to the Indian Ocean World (*ibid.*). According to Kessler (2006), such cultural pattern is known as Swahili civilization that started with the arrival of Arab traders along the East

African coast in the 1400s. As long as they established trade routes farther into interior, Swahili trading culture spread together with development of Kiswahili language (*ibid.*).

Nonetheless, such successful maritime trade links were raided by Portuguese who conquered many coastal urban areas so as to capture gold from Sofala [(Zimbabwe) *ibid.*]. Portuguese raids disrupted and disordered many centuries' urban outstanding trade links and they were driven into almost two and a half centuries of poverty (*ibid.*). It is argued that such Portuguese conquest along the Indian Ocean coast facilitated for other subjugations in the eighteenth century, for Europeans utilised the coast's economy, like the French who started exporting slaves, while in 1698, Omani forces conquered Zanzibar and made its centre of power in the Indian Ocean (*ibid.*).

In another vein, Swahili coast rebuilt coastal trade in the next half of the eighteenth century whereby they obtained ivory as well as slaves in exchange for cloth, hardware, dates, munitions and valuable metals and later in 1784 as well as 1785, growth of wealth paved the way for the Sultan of Oman to occupy Kilwa (in south-eastern Tanzania) so as to capture its trade (*ibid.*). By then, particularly in eighteenth and nineteenth centuries, merchants carried out caravan trade with the interior with human porters like Wayao, Wanyamwezi, Wakimba and Wasumbwa (*ibid.*). It is informed that Wayao from Lake Malawi shores sent slaves to the coast thereby linked the Indian Ocean coast after trade disruption by Portuguese invasion (*ibid.*). Moreover, in the 1720s, Wasagara migrations, availability of natural resources, central location of Wanyamwezi together with seasonal trading organization encouraged Wanyamwezi porters to start caravan trade organization (Rockel, 2006; Unangst, 2015). It is argued that such trade grew fast because Wanyamwezi and Arab traders instituted links based on their commercial interest with Arab traders who built major settlements at several places like Tabora in Tabora region and Ujiji in Kigoma region, while political power including labour control remained in Wanyamwezi rulers (Unangst, 2015).

The reported caravan trade fashioned conditions for development of wage labour before European arrival because Wanyamwezi carried out their own culture of free wage labour and thus, they controlled wages as well as working conditions in caravan trade even after European explorers and traders started participating (*ibid.*). In 1840s, the central route to Lake Victoria was opened and later on the network of routes as well as stops stabilized, which meant that establishment of caravan trade integrated such areas into the world economy for coastal traders, for instance, Wanyamwezi with political leaders who charged tolls to passing caravans, all became wealthy (*ibid.*).

Several historians express caravan trade and its outcomes as the most important developments in realm of cultural diversity in nineteenth century East Africa, for instance, in 1997, Jutta Bückendorf described a "century of upheaval" in East Africa before German colonialists arrived (Unangst, 2015), while John Iliffe (1979) called it a period of "structural change" in economics. Increased social tensions together with economic changes with several influences from inside and outside the East African area extremely altered economic as well as political organization (Unangst, 2015).

Furthermore, in Tanzania, wealth accumulated in port towns as merchants traded with regions to the west, for instance, Tanga and Pangani ports traded with Kilimanjaro region, while along the coast (in the south and north of Dar es Salaam), people of Saadani, Bagamoyo, and Mbwamaji traded with the central route and Kilwa traded with the south (*ibid.*). In Zanzibar, rulers by then, the Sultans, had no direct control over the mainland and thus, it had power of a "commercial empire" that produced goods for export on Unguja and Pemba isles and traded beyond and beyond west through time (*ibid.*). The then Sultan of Zanzibar, Barghash bin Said, who ruled from 1870 to 1888, built a western-trained army and naval force under British supervision and increased his power in northern coastal towns of mainland Tanzania (Pangani and Saadani) and stationed troops in Bagamoyo and Dar es Salaam (*ibid.*). By the early 1880s, leaders as far west as the Great Lakes saw Zanzibar as the central point of the East Central African regions (*ibid.*). Trade from main harbours along the coast, Bagamoyo, Kilwa and Pangani furnished Zanzibar sultans with economic advantages of capture (*ibid.*).

Following East Africa's integration to the world economy in the nineteenth century, a notable development happened. Accordingly, slavery became highly widespread (*ibid.*). Moreover, plantation agriculture and slavery gradually developed along the coast during the century and sprawled west along caravan routes (*ibid.*).

From 1870s onwards, 70 kilometres north of Dar es Salaam, Bagamoyo became the main port for export of ivory, slavery as well as gum copal and they paid to Wazaramo rulers (local leaders) to the town's west in exchange for permitting caravans to pass through (*ibid.*). Zanzibar posted officials in each coastal town to administer tolls and periodically dispatched troops to uphold control over trade whenever it was indispensable (*ibid.*). In the nineteenth century, traders who were foreigners, in particular, Indian traders migrated to the coast in considerable numbers and one merchant, Sewa Haji, dominated the trading community of Bagamoyo from the 1870s to the late 1890s by supplying Arab, African, and European caravans with trade goods including porters and bought ivory they took to the coast (*ibid.*). Sewa Haji had representatives at main towns of the interior but important to note is that from 1870s to 1880s, Zanzibari traders controlled trade deep into the interior, in search for people to enslave and elephants to hunt (*ibid.*).

In other developments, the then Zanzibar Sultan, Sultan Majid regularly paid to upper-class members of coastal society to recognize his rule and made a kind of state organ, while the later Sultan, Sultan Bargash had a political representative in Tabora (central-western Tanzania), the main trading town that became an important Arab outpost because Unyanyembe was the most receptive chiefdom to Arab settlement (*ibid.*). The Zanzibar Sultanate held its position in trade with the interior in its treaties with European traders as well as governments thereby it ensured a state monopoly over trade in ivory and copra (*ibid.*). Besides, Arab traders were incorporated into local politics there, but upheld links to Zanzibar and from the middle of the nineteenth century, traders from the coast gained big advantage in trade as the ivory limit moved west, they settled along the caravan routes and they secured long-term credit from Zanzibar (*ibid.*).

After a failed involvement in a war in Unyamwezi in the early 1870s, Sultan Barghash mainly left politics in the Great Lakes area and several local rulers appeared in the late nineteenth century with military control of the caravan routes (*ibid.*). Newly emerged rulers were incorporated in the world economy (*ibid.*). They integrated through trade and international networks and as a result, traders rushed to Ujiji (Kigoma) in the 1860s and 1870s as the ivory border moved west (*ibid.*).

Therefore, trade brought coastal merchants and African associates into daily contact, mainly around Tabora and Ujiji towns (*ibid.*). Through the second half of the nineteenth century, migrants went to the coast to work in new industries, trade and plantation. In another developmental process, Kiswahili spread as the language of central and northern caravan trade routes, but it was not the only language of trade (*ibid.*). Other languages included Kiyao along the southern caravan trade route and Kinyamwezi of the western plateau caravan trade route (*ibid.*).

Importantly, an administrative class, trained in an Islamic education system, developed on the coast in the second half of the nineteenth century and Islamic education was prestigious in coastal society (*ibid.*). In further developments, the trade boom amplified access to signs of status inland that led to competition to prove one's generosity and links to overseas areas (*ibid.*). Significantly, cultural elements from many various societies in East Africa, Swahili, Zanzibari, Wanyamwezi, Wamanyema, Wazaramo, Wayao and others became part of the culture of journey (*ibid.*).

This shows the manner there was cultural adoption by several ethnic groups along caravan trade links/routes in the country and thus, depicted cultural diversity. Some of the ethnic groups rallied with foreign traders as receptive interactions, while others were non-receptive. However, there were hostilities between several ethnic groups due to civil wars as it is presented in subsequent paragraphs.

On the other hand, local people built power through control over resources or travel along trade routes and used links with the coast to build their own political power and deployed signs of ethnic identity (*ibid.*). The said rulers used trade goods to build followers and armed their men with firearms, for example, Ntemi in Kinyamwezi or Chief Mirambo, Mnyamwezi ruler, dominated the area between Tabora, Lake Tanganyika, and Lake Victoria from the 1870s through the early 1880s by building up his military power and capacity to raid his neighbours (*ibid.*). Mirambo played Arab merchants and European missionaries for his own needs and after he lost a war with Unyanyembe and Tabora over trade in 1876, he attempted to build direct links with European traders (*ibid.*). Other areas had their political systems too. For example, Wahaya and Wasukuma in northwest Tanzania had centralized political institutions based on ritual kinship before German arrival (Unangst, 2015).

In another vein, areas southeast of Lake Victoria had constant warfare with no central political institutions (*ibid.*). Areas immediately to the southwest of the coast experienced unrest in the 1860s and 1870s as Wangoni migrants moved there from South Africa (*ibid.*). Along northern coastal areas, such as west of Bagamoyo, Pangani, and Saadani were dominated by Waseguha who expanded their power through slave raids using firearms traded through Zanzibar (*ibid.*).

In the central part of the country, Wagogo controlled trade through organization of water along dry parts of the central caravan trade route, while along the northern coast, particularly Tanga region, Shambaa kingdom of Usambara drew compliment from the coastal towns (*ibid.*). Nonetheless, between 1860s and late 1880s, Shambaa kingdom was wrecked by civil war, but finally, Semboja won the war and built associations with traders to increase trade as well as his power (*ibid.*).

To the west of Shambaa kingdom, there were Wapare societies that fell apart due to attacks by Wamaasai and slave raiders, while in Tabora, Wanyamwezi rulers managed to copy Wangoni military organization to dominate interior trade (*ibid.*). Chiefs Swetu and Fundikira built Unyanyembe to the most powerful political body in the first half of the nineteenth century (*ibid.*). On the other hand, in the northeast near Mount Kilimanjaro, Wachagga societies were split into many different kingdoms, whereas in Arusha region, Wamaasai societies fought frequent wars against one another and others (*ibid.*).

There were notable scenarios too in southern Tanzania. Wangoni, Wayao and Wahehe formed the main economic and political powers in the second half of the nineteenth century (*ibid.*). Accordingly, there were Wangoni migrations from southern Africa who formed a formidable new political balance, for their warriors under the rubric *ruga ruga* raided surrounding regions and created a military basis for political power that became the model for state building throughout central Tanzania, for example, the chiefs of Unyanyembe in Tabora (*ibid.*). It was reported that ruga ruga warriors formed new levels of violence across areas they passed through, for instance, Munyigumba unified Wahehe around the middle of the nineteenth century, which eventually led to domination of the central trade route between Tabora and Kilosa in Morogoro region (*ibid.*). In another vein, Wayao societies moved too into southern Tanzania from Mozambique and became the main mediators in ivory and slave trades in Kilwa Kisiwani and Kilwa Kivinje (*ibid.*). By the 1870s, they conducted their own raids such that their language, Kiyao, became the principal trade language in southern Tanzania (*ibid.*).

However, over the nineteenth century, cultural diversity changed from local people with Arabian and Indian interactions to Europeans. In Tanzania, like elsewhere in East Africa, European countries with their merchants changed undertakings of the maritime trade whereby other vessels that never sailed using seasonal wind changes, particularly steam ships allowed for trade outside of the monsoon season (*ibid.*). The telegraph permitted for fast communication about changes in world markets, the Suez Canal allowed for much faster transit between Europe and the Ocean and European maps rationalized the Ocean's spaces (*ibid.*). Nonetheless, local trade remained to traders who carried goods by dhow but the 1870s witnessed a highly intrusive European presence and there was further British pressure against slave trade together with additional Zanzibari efforts to increase state power (*ibid.*).

In other developments, missionaries got into East Africa including Tanzania and thus, changed the already established local people's cultural interactions with Arabs and Indians. Therefore, missionaries marked establishment of Christianity at varying dimensions that included resistances. For example, the Church Missionary Society (CMS) and the Catholic White Fathers established grips in Buganda in the 1870s with the White Fathers founded, particularly to tend to East Africa, after the Primate of Africa, Charles Lavigerie, called for further attention to the region (*ibid.*).

Besides, Catholic missions sought to put Africans into Christianity and to what they conceived as civilization and later on by 1884, five missionary societies were established during German East Africa colonial era (*ibid.*). But before German colonial rule, the following missionary stations or centres were set up: the Holy Ghost Fathers were established at Bagamoyo in 1868, they built a station inland at Mhonda in 1877; White Fathers built a station in Ujiji (Kigoma) in 1879; the Anglican Universities Mission had stations at Magila (Tanga region) and Masasi (Mtwara region); the Church Missionary Society had a station at Mpwapwa (Dodoma region) after 1876; and the London Missionary Society had a centre at Mirambo (Tabora region) after 1878 (*ibid.*).

Accordingly, such missionary stations converted people to Christianity (*ibid.*). In the 1850s, Germans had first entered societies and markets of East Africa, when the Hamburg trading houses, namely, O'Swald and Hansing established posts on Unguja Island to trade European manufactured goods for ivory (*ibid.*). Initial Hansa traders incorporated into existing trade links (*ibid.*).

Of special note is that illicit interactions that affected local people seized to continue due to missionary works. For example, slavery was abolished by Missionaries who assumed free people in their stations. They converted them to Christianity. Later on, with German colonial rule, slavery was abolished.

Interactions between local people and Germans are manifest through further development of Kiswahili language, particularly lexicography, which is first associated with Arabs together with their ambitions to expand their trade influences on the east coast of Africa (*ibid.*). There are records that provide evidence of letters written in Kiswahili that date by the year 1300 with use of Arabic script (*ibid.*). Later on, European missionaries in search for considerable political grip and control in East Africa were at the forefront in cementing their interactions with local people through use of the already developed Kiswahili (*ibid.*). Notably, as will be presented in subsequent parts, development of Kiswahili language involved local languages that included Kiyao, Kingoni, Kinyamwezi and Kigogo, while foreign languages, particularly Arabic later blended Bantu words with Arabic to form Kiswahili with integration of few Germany words like *schule* as well as *baiskili* (thus, known in Kiswahili as *shule* and *baiskeli*) that led to further development of Kiswahili by missionaries (notably, Dr. Ludwig Krapf and John Rebman).

Furthermore, additional interactions were amplified through missionaries' social services provision to local people. Accordingly, it must be underscored that appearance of Christian missionaries in the nineteenth century brought about establishment of social services that included schools, hospitals and a great need to convert Africans into Christianity (Kessler, 2006). Thus, many missionaries established themselves in several places in the country and imparted skills including experience to undertake several works with Europeans (*ibid.*).

However, important aspects to note include the fact that Christianity was brought by missionaries who totally changed African cultural life ways. Such changes were witnessed through abolition of traditional African religions. Also, there was total abolition of monogamy for both societal forms, whether patrilineal or matrilineal.

Another important cultural diversity to note is that Germany missionaries were instrumental in sowing seeds of occupation (colonialism) to Tanzania as manifest through their Kiswahili language interactions that later on smoothed German colonial rulers. The first such Kiswahili works from German missionaries is testified in the mid-nineteenth century, whereby German missionary, Dr. Ludwig Krapf published Kiswahili grammar in 1850 (Unangst, 2015). Also, in the same year, he published a Kiswahili word list that had equivalents in the following East African languages: Kiswahili, Kinika, Kikamba, Kipokomo, Kihiau and Kigalla (*ibid.*). Then in 1882, Krapf released the first Kiswahili-English dictionary titled, 'Dictionary of the Suahili Language' (*ibid.*). As a result, Krapf and his associate, Rev. Rebmann and the dictionary itself, were sources that were referenced by their contemporaries and future Kiswahili language researchers (*ibid.*).

The interactions to further crafting as well as development of German language and Kiswahili language, Prof. C. Velten printed a two-volume dictionary, Suaheli-Deutsch in 1910 and Deutsch-Suaheli in 1933 (*ibid.*). Therefore, the terminal nineteenth century and the onset of the twentieth century was a period dominated by missionary publications that included compilation of many dictionaries (*ibid.*).

"Amongst those of note are the following: Dictionnaire français-kisouahili authored by Father Dutrieux in 1880, Vocabulaire français-kiswahili et kiswahili-français written by the White Fathers (Père Blancs) in 1885, authors of a Swahili-Latin dictionary; grammar book with a German-Swahili dictionary, Praktische Grammatick der Suaheli-Sprache auch für den Selbstunterricht. Mit Nebungstücken, einem Lesebuche und einem Deutsch-Kisuaheli Wörtebuch by August Seidel from 1890 or a similar paper authored by Friedrich von Nettlebladt in 1891 [(Hendrix 1982)" *ibid.*: 417].

Aspects to note on success or failure of cultural diversity in Tanzania are evident through German travellers/explorers, missionaries and business entities. For example, in 1874, ivory-focused trading house, namely, Heinrich Adolph Meyer, joined O'Swald and Hansing trading houses and by the way of diversity, particularly socio-economic interactions, pre-colonial German travellers as well as traders depended on local logistical support including knowledge in travelling through East Africa (*ibid.*) They were one of several foreign elements involved in caravan trade that drew East Africa into the world economic system (*ibid.*).

In recapitulation, Germans were not the first foreign group to get involved in East Africa, politically and economically, because the nineteenth century in the region was, obviously, a time of great disorder (*ibid.*). Increasing demand for ivory in world markets and slaves in Zanzibar, progressively incorporated areas as far west as the Great Lakes into the world capitalist economy and fashioned something of a unified economic system over the track of the century (*ibid.*). Nonetheless, it must be noted that the economic system was not politically unified and notwithstanding, Zanzibari claims to a huge empire, the coast and the interior developed diverse political bodies (*ibid.*). They evidenced the rise of centralized power structures that went into conflict in the last few decades before German colonization and therefore, German colonists arrived in a region in chaos and transition that took over German capitalist companies that failed to carry on with their trades (*ibid.*).

2.3 Interactions during colonialism

Colonialism in Eastern African territories (including Tanganyika, the current mainland Tanzania) started through German enterprises that were protected by the Imperial German government. Such measure was carried out on 27th February 1885 through issuance of a letter of protection (*Schutzbrief*) by the Imperial German government to the German East Africa Company [(Deutsch-Ostafrikanische Gesellschaft, DOAG) Unangst, 2015]. Such letter of protection was conclusion of the DOAG's campaign to found a German overseas colony following the company [under its previous formation, Society for German Colonization (Gesellschaft für deutsche Kolonisation, GfdK)] that carried out an expedition to Usagara in East Africa to acquire territory, whose members (Carl Peters, Joachim Graf von Pfeil, and Karl Jühlke) signed a series of treaties with local men and women they called "sultans" who gave up sovereign rights to territory to the German expedition (*ibid.*).

Of special note is that such signed treaties (or special documents) involved people who were illiterate. Thus, they were lured to agree to an issue that was used in German legal parlance, signing papers as authentic agreements. Such measures denigrated Tanzanians' right to self-rule they had before, right to land ownership and many other rights.

The treaties and other maltreatments to local people provided room for negative cultural interactions by Germans against local people who had their own legitimate local leaderships. For example, according to Pizzo (2007: 45), such legally and morally delicate "… documents became the basis for the authority of Peters' Deutsch Ostafrikanische Gesellschaft (German East Africa Company) and, by extension, of the German Reich" whereby instead of establishment of political firmness in local areas, Carl Peters stretched destruction by plundering villages, set ablaze houses and smashed anything that never burnt (*ibid.*). Notably, Carl Peters left a legend whereby Germans and local Tanzanian people's interactions as major examples of brutality as well as incompetence of German imperialism in Africa (*ibid.*). Other explorers like Henry Morton Stanley (known to Africans as Bula Mutari, breaker of stones) and other explorers of the 1860s to 1880s in Tanzania and elsewhere in Africa were indulged in innumerable instances of abuse, violence and unpleasant behaviours, which resulted in deaths of numerous Africans (*ibid.*).

The German Chancellor, Bismarck, hoped that DOAG would be an effective as well as inexpensive method of colonizing East Africa but never materialised because from 1885 to 1888, the company was on business collapse and was almost bankrupt amidst Arab resistance (*ibid.*). By 1889, almost every community in coastal East Africa revolted against company authority (*ibid.*). The revolts compelled the chancellor to exercise brutality by deploying mercenaries from Egypt who applied brutality that suppressed the coast, destroyed many villages, razed urban settlements, hanged as well as shot many Africans and drove away groups of revolts led by Arabs (Hari and Bushiri) who surrendered to the mercenaries and were hung (*ibid.*). Many captured Africans were killed by hanging or shooting (*ibid.*). There are several places with trees believed to have been used as hanging trees in Tanzania, for example, in Mwanza, Bagamoyo, Songea and several other places.

Thus, before colonialism by the Imperial German Government, the company raced for colonies and strived for acquiring territories through dispatch of several expeditions in East Africa (*ibid.*). In due regard, the company used treaties to create a private empire for the benefit of the German nation (*ibid.*).

In 1885, the Germans claimed Tanganyika to be a colony at the Berlin Conference but they were brutal (Kessler, 2006). In another stance, their rule was of short duration that left long lasting impacts like development of cash crops for exports that included sisal, coffee and cotton (Bourguignon, 2018). Other notable positive impacts encompassed start of construction of the railroad network from the east in Dar es Salaam harbour to Kigoma on the west, institution of harbours at Dar es Salaam as well as Tanga along the coast and in Kigoma too, an administrative structure as collectors of revenue (essentially labour taxation) and start of an educational system (*ibid.*). Besides, the colonial regime "... left an original structure of production of export crops where African peasant farming coexisted with a limited number of large plantations managed by European settlers" (*ibid.*: 2). On the other hand, such rule disrupted traditional agriculture that led to impoverishment, population decline in some areas, and spread of tsetse flies (*ibid.*: 3).

Bagomoyo, 70 kilometres north of Dar es Salaam was the first headquarters of German East Africa Company. However, in 1891, Dar es Salaam became their headquarters such that in subsequent three decades, German rule laid the foundation for urban governance and resource access in Dar es Salaam with house structures including the state house in Dar es Salaam as Germany heritage in Tanzania (Bryceson, 2010).

The Germany legacy is manifest through built heritage around the country, there are several buildings left by colonialists in several areas like Tabora, Kigoma, Morogoro, Lushoto with Governor's Lodge at Magamba

(Tanga), Dodoma, Mwanza (buildings and hanging area), Songea (with hanging area) and many other places. Dar es Salaam city has many buildings including the state house and several others along streets along with several areas that include Samora Avenue, Shabaan Robert, Garden Street, Mnazi Mmoja Grounds and National Stadium (Kisusi, 2014). Other buildings include those housing missionaries like White Fathers' Building and Azania Front Lutheran Cathedral Church Kivukoni, Saint Joseph's Cathedral (Catholic Archdiocese of Dar es Salaam), City Council Offices, Old Boma building and many others (*ibid.*)

However, in another vein, an impact worthy of recalling involved the Germans' rule of the country that was brutal (Kessler, 2006). As a result, the Germans had to fight fierce resistances by local people that started from 1905 and lasted in 1907 (*ibid.*).

Essentially, there are marked economic developments through established cotton as well as sisal plantations during German colonial rule including development of infrastructure that benefit the country, to date. Such developments show the manner the country started to be integrated into cash crops economy and thus, into export of agricultural produce to the world markets. All such economic developments by Germans are still benefitting Tanzania. Moreover, construction works that included the central railway together with road networks that are still operating up to now are additional economic benefits enjoyed by the country.

On the other hand, the said plantations and development of infrastructure during German colonial rule had negative interactions that led into a very big strife or war. For example, people revolted due to forced labour with either low or no wages including unjust taxation and corporal punishment (Rushohora & Kurmann, 2017; Gregory, 2020). As a result, on 15th July, 1905, war erupted at Nandete village in Matumbi land/Ngindo areas in Kilwa District, Lindi region and ended at Mahenge area in Songea in 1907 where the Germans defeated local fighters (Gregory, 2020). Reasons for such war outbreak involved a revolt against German agricultural policy in what came to be called the Majimaji Rebellion and later on, it was renamed by post-independent Tanzania as Majimaji war (*ibid.*).

But later on in 1914, World War I (WW I) broke out (Bourguignon, 2018). The war involved intense local fighting against the British and Belgian forces in Africa (*ibid.*). After the end of WWI, the Germans lost and the British were mandated to rule Tanganyika [(now mainland Tanzania) *ibid.*].

2.4 Interactions during post-independence of Tanzania, to date

2.4.1 Religious undertakings

As already presented, cultural diversity through religious indoctrination to local people was brought by Arabs through Islam and Europeans, especially German missionaries through Christianity. However, such religious indoctrination did not wipe out believers in traditional African religions who currently, form minority groups in the country. They existed and they still exist due to the post-independent country's adoption of United Nations Universal Declaration on Human Rights whereby it permits people's freedom of worship as long as they do not infringe or jeopardize one's religious belief, whether conventional or traditional.

Concerning social institution, some notable changes happened. Although the family is still the basic unit, cultural diversity is markedly changed in Tanzania. For instance, while Christianity abandoned polygamy, Islam and traditional African religions still embrace polygamy.

2.4.2 Language interactions (Kiswahili language)

An extremely important aspect on cultural diversity pertains to language of communication, Kiswahili that was developed by Arabs and amplified by German missionaries. It continued to be used by people as means of communication for long distance trade, colonial government undertakings and it was used for religious teachings, Islam and Christian. Thereafter, as a further unifying factor, during independence struggles that were through dialogue, stewarded by Mwalimu Julius Kambarage Nyerere who became the first president of independent Tanganyika (now mainland Tanzania and then through union with Zanzibar, Tanzania), Kiswahili language was largely used. It was a unifying factor during struggles for independence and president Nyerere endorsed as well as mandated Kiswahili language to be an official and national language.

Besides, Mwalimu Nyerere's dealing with three archenemies he identified to wage war against, namely, ignorance, poverty and diseases believed that they could be wiped out first through education. Accordingly, he mandated language of instruction at elementary level to be Kiswahili. It is a requirement that is still in force. Accordingly, with moves of using Kiswahili language as an official and national language, the language has become the biggest binding force for all people of all walks of life from different religious denominations and ethnic groups in the country. As a result, people inhabit at any part of the republic and they marry who ever, regardless of religious or ethnic affiliation. Therefore, Kiswahili language is the biggest unifying factor for all people in the country and set the country unique in terms of cultural underpinnings that make it a safe haven in Africa against over a hundred and twenty ethnic groups. Most importantly, Germans who amplified Kiswahili are still embracing the language whereby several universities in Germany are offering Kiswahili degree programmes.

2.4.3 Social services delivery

Pertaining to missionary works from pre-colonial times to date, there are landmark developments that cement cultural interactions. Missionary works under Lutheran and Catholic denominations have facilitated expansion of all areas of social services to the highest level. For example, there are Zonal Referral Hospitals, namely, Kilimanjaro Christian Medical Centre in Moshi under Lutherans and Bugando Medical Centre in Mwanza city under Catholics that operate with no religious discrimination. Moreover, missionaries saw the seed for both formal education and religious education that paved the way for local Tanzanians to be players including assumption of leadership roles in religious institutions and government as well as political institutions.

2.4.4 Training and Exchange of Expertise

For quite some time since independence, the German Government, through German Academic Exchange Services (DAAD) and others, has been offering scholarships for training for academicians and technicians, respectively, at universities and government offices in ministries and public entities. Moreover, there are exchange programmes between German and Tanzanian scholars at public as well as private universities. Academic members of staff and students have been taking part in exchange programmes in the two countries. For example, there are exchange programmes between Saint Augustine University of Tanzania (SAUT) and University of Vechta as well as other universities in Tanzania. Trainings involve fields in Social Sciences, Laws, Engineering, the Humanities, Business Studies and many others. Such training and exchange programmes involve both genders.

2.4.5 Research and Development

The German government, through German Technical Cooperation Agency (GTZ) has long time and long standing programmes in agricultural research for development of coconut farming along the coastal (and eastern) strip of Tanzania. Many Tanzanian and German experts have been working at both countries in training, research and development of agriculture at various centres in the country. Additionally, there are long time and long standing research and conservation of wildlife areas such as Ngorongoro Conservation Area Authority (NCAA), Serengeti National Park, Rubondo Island National Park, Tanzania Wildlife Research Institute (TAWIRI) collaborations with Frankfurt Zoological Society. Importantly, all research and development endeavours are in line with the country's goals of dealing with gender equity and inequality whereby participation is earmarked for both sexes and without any prejudice pertaining to one's ethnic affiliation, religious orientation and many other aspects.

2.4.6 Democracy, Gender Equality and Human Rights

The country's constitution (1977 and its amendments of 1984) contains articles dealing with human rights, including protection of the integrity of its citizens. In 2000, the country reaffirmed its commitment to reducing gender inequalities by recognizing goals of the United Nations Millennium Declaration (Deotti and Estruch, 2016). Tanzania ratified key international and regional protocols related to gender equality and women's empowerment (GEWE), committing to respect gender equality and uphold democratic rights (URT, 2016). Besides, the National Women and Gender Development Policy of 2000 (amended in 2003) and the National Gender Development Strategy of 2005 were formulated (URT, 2005). All provide guidelines for governmental and non-governmental actors to incorporate gender equality concerns into all their plans, strategies, programs and budgets (*ibid.*).

Furthermore, Tanzania formulated legal instruments on the rights of women that include the Sexual Offences Special Provision Act of 1998 (SOSPA); the Convention on the Elimination of All forms of Discrimination Against Women (CEDAW); and the Protocol to the African Charter on Human and Peoples' Rights on the Rights of Women in Africa [(Maputo Protocol) *op cit.*]. Besides, the government of Tanzania permitted establishment of private legal agencies to solely provide legal assistance to women that include Tanzania

Women Lawyers Association (Tanzania Women Lawyers Association (TAWLA); Tanzania Media Women's Association (Tanzania Media Women's Association (TAMWA); and Women's Legal Aid Centre [(WLAC) *ibid.*].

Accordingly, the country observes all tenets imbued in observation of democracy and human rights whereby gender equality is considered and highly practiced at bureaucratic, political and public institutional levels. The country observes the quota system for political positions for women like for Members of Parliament and Councillors while at the same time, all genders are equally considered to be voted in all political posts they wish to vie for.

Concerning Good Governance, Faith-inspired organizations (FIOs) involve the Tanzanian government on issues of governance, corruption and civic engagement (International Partnership on Religion and Sustainable Development, 2019). For instance, in 2009 and 2010, the Konrad Adenauer Stiftung and World Conference on Religion and Peace/IRCPT convened interfaith meetings in Dar es Salaam to discuss the role of religious leaders in promoting civic education and contributing to the political process (*ibid.*).

On the other hand, development partners take part in government efforts that are geared towards fulfilment of observance of democracy and human rights. For example, Friedrich Ebert Stiftung, a Germany entity, has been at the forefront in promotion of democracy and human rights for Non-Governmental Organizations and political parties in Tanzania.

2.4.7 Economic and Infrastructure Development

The German colonial government amplified and intensified plantation agriculture and thus, promoted cash crop economy. Such ventures involved cotton and sisal plantation. Besides, there were construction works of roads in Dar es Salaam including Tanga harbour developments and construction of the central railway from Dar es Salaam along the Indian Ocean to Kigoma in the west at Lake Tanganyika shores. Moreover, due to economic growth including development of infrastructure, plantation economy together with construction of government administrative buildings including private buildings like churches, there emerged small settlements in some places that developed further into urban settlements around the country. That was evident as the first German East African headquarters at Bagamoyo in late nineteenth century that was shifted to Dar es Salaam in 1890.

Through time, from colonial rule to post-independent Tanzania and currently, the country is upgrading economic development in terms of expansion of cash crops through export businesses and some local processing of raw cotton into textile industries. Taxation system initiated by Germans has been upgraded by the post-independent government and is fully useful to the central government's revenue.

In another vein, growth of urban areas or urbanism was facilitated by former collective settlements established from German colonial rule to date. Such settlements were facilitated through unified medium of communication, Kiswahili language that was initiated by Arabs and later on, developed further by German missionaries. Hence, they facilitated people to leave in small urban or collective settlements without any discrimination, regardless of gender and/or ethnic origin.

2.4.8 Diplomatic Relations

Diplomatic relations are facilitating long standing collaborations in the country. There are established embassies in Dar es Salaam for Germany Embassy and in Berlin for Tanzanian Embassy, all show continued cultural ties with the two countries at such a high level of collaboration.

Accordingly, diplomatic relations facilitate interactions, movements of people between the two countries. There are peoples' movements from the two countries. Nonetheless, visa processes for Tanzanians are somehow cumbersome. For instance, categories for visa processing do not include academic (for studies and research) and academics are treated like business travellers. Moreover, visa processing is complicated by being outsourced to a foreigner who does not respect local cultural aspects like disrespect, mishandling visa applicants and return of passport already processed from the Germany Embassy is prone to harassment, especially if one outsources an express courier that they already recommend. This shows the manner there is inequality of cultural diversity for movements between Tanzanians and Germans whereby Tanzanians, especially academics are ill-treated by the visa vendor outsourced by the Germany government.

On the positive aspect pertaining to cultural diversity, the Germany Embassy has and still is making great collaborations on various socio-economic services at diverse capacities. For instance, the Germany government has been up-grading and funding military works like Military Hospitals in Dar es Salaam and Tabora. The German Government has been providing notable financial grants to Tanzania for various development programmes. Accordingly, on behalf of the German Federal Government,

KfW is supporting Tanzania on health, social protection and population policy; and it is protecting the natural basis for livelihoods. Furthermore, on behalf of the Federal Ministry for Economic Cooperation and Development (BMZ), KfW is contributing to financing the Tanzanian national health insurer, National Health Insurance Fund (NHIF) by offering free insurance for poor pregnant women and their newborns hereby helping to reduce maternal as well as infant mortality and prevent maternal and infant illnesses including disabilities. Additionally, KfW is supporting construction of a mother-and-child clinic in Dar es Salaam, which specialises in high-risk pregnancies and neonatal care.

Moreover, on behalf of the German Federal Government, KfW is financing supply of safe drinking water and better sanitation services for over 800,000 people in five regional towns of Lindi, Mtwara, Kigoma, Sumbawanga and Babati.

To preserve the country's unparalleled biodiversity, KfW supports several UNESCO-recognised World Heritage Sites, including Serengeti National Park. It provides Tanzanian partners with funds for better equipping administrative bodies of protected area. Besides, KfW promotes construction of public infrastructure, new income opportunities and participatory land use planning in outskirts of national parks. The measures include designating usage zones in which sustainable hunting and logging are permitted.

2.5 Concluding Remarks

This chapter on Cultural Diversity in Tanzania and Germany highlights too other aspects on diversity. For example, gender diversity including interactions, are underscored in the presentation. Continued cultural diversity is seen from the beginning during pre-colonialism, during colonialism and post-independence to date. The initial era facilitated installation and thus, continued as well as sustenance of existing positive cultural diversity aspects. For example, Kiswahili language that was initiated by Arabs by incorporating words from local ethnic groups, essentially Bantu population groups was further developed and refined by Germany missionaries (Dr. Ludwig Krapf and Reverend John Rebman) who wrote Kiswahili dictionary. Language as a medium of culture is important for human beings' sake or livelihoods and thus, such continued use of Kiswahili language facilitated smooth dialogues and other independence (*uhuru* in Kiswahili) struggles for Tanzania that were successful over 120 ethnic groups in the country. Moreover, Kiswahili language is the national and official language of communication that additionally make people maintain peace and security in the country. Such stance, along with other government measures, makes Tanzania the haven of peace in Africa as a whole.

Furthermore, economic undertakings like plantation farming of cotton and sisal established by the Germany colonial government have been carried out by the independent government. Currently, along with other additional cash crops, the country facilitates cash crop farming. Also, taxation system initiated by Germans is carried over and expanded to in-fill government coffers as revenue to run fundamental government affairs.

The Germans constructed infrastructure like the central railway (that was completed in 1907), sea ports (Dar es Salaam and Tanga) and several roads in the country are still in use for transportation of goods in the country and overseas. All such foundations are benefitting the independent government thereby facilitating continued interactions not only with Germans but also with others around the world.

Moreover, missionaries established social services that included hospitals and schools. Health and education services have been expanded during independent Tanzania. For example, there are zonal referral hospitals that resulted from initial ordinary health facilities established by missionaries. Thus, health, education, good governance, democracy, gender equality, human rights as well as political matters in Tanzania (public as well as private) in all dimensions are still enjoying from collaborations with the Germany government and institutions, private and public.

References

Becker, Felicitas (2004). "Traders, 'Big men' and Prophets: Political Continuity and Crisis in the Maji Maji Rebellion in Southeast Tanzania." *Journal of African History.* 45: 1 – 22. DOI: 10.1017/S0021853703008545.

Bourguignon, François (2018) "Political and economic development of Tanzania: A Brief Survey – Tanzania Institutional Diagnostic." In Economic Development and Institutions. 1 – 39. London: EDI.

Bryceson, Deborah Fahy (2010). "Dar es Salaam as a 'harbour of peace' in East Africa: Tracing the role of creolized urban ethnicity in nation-state formation," WIDER Working Paper, No. 2010/19, ISBN 978-92-9230-254-2, The United Nations University World Institute for Development Economics Research (UNU-WIDER), Helsinki.

Deotti, Laura and Estruch, Elisenda (2016). *Addressing rural youth migration at its root causes: A conceptual framework*. Rome: Food and Agriculture Organization of the United Nations.

Elijah, G. (2010). "Making History: Historical Narratives of the Maji Maji." Penn History Review, 17(2), 60–77.

Giblin, J., & Monson, J. (Eds). (2010). *Maji Maji Lifting the Frog of War*. Leiden, Boston: Brill.

Gregory, Athanasy (2020). "The Role of Women in Maji Maji War from 1905 to 1907 in Matumbiland, Ngindo and Ngoniland War Zones, Tanzania." East African Journal of Education and Social Sciences. 1(3): 52-59. DOI: https://doi.org/10.46606/eajess2020v01i03.0042 URL: http://eajess.ac.tz

Iliffe, John. (1979). *A Modern History of Tanganyika*. Cambridge: Cambridge University Press.

International Partnership on Religion and Sustainable Development (2019). Faith and Development in focus - Tanzania. Berkley: World Faiths Development Dialogue Berkley Center for Religion, Peace & World Affairs.

Kessler, Ilana, R. (2006). "What Went Right in Tanzania: How Nation Building and Political Culture Have Produced Forty-Four Years of Peace." Thesis Submitted in Partial Fulfilment of the Requirements for the Award of Honours in International Politics and the African Studies Certificate in the Edmund A. Walsh School of Foreign Service of Georgetown University.

Kisusi, Rahel Lucas (2014). Promoting Public Awareness on the Existing Cultural Heritage Tourism Sites: A Case of Dar es Salaam City. MA Dissertation, Open University of Tanzania.

Kottak, Conrad Phillip (2004). Anthropology: The Exploration of Human Diversity. 10th ED. New York: McGraw-Hill Companies.

LeGall, Yann (2020). "Songea Mbano and the 'halfway dead' of the Majimaji War (1905–7) in memory and theatre." *Human Remains and Violence*. 6(2): 4–22. http://dx.doi.org/10.7227/HRV.6.2.2

Lin, Cong (2019). "Understanding Cultural Diversity and Diverse Identities. In W. Leal Filho et al. (eds.), Quality Education, Encyclopedia of the UN Sustainable Development Goals, pp 1-10. Switzerland: Springer Nature AG. https://doi.org/10.1007/978-3-319-69902-8_37-1

Pizzo, David (2007). "To Devour the Land of Mkwawa:" Colonial Violence and the German-Hehe War in East Africa c. 1884-1914." A dissertation for the degree of Doctor of Philosophy in the Department of History, University of North Carolina at Chapel Hill.

Rockel, Stephen, J. (2006). *Carriers of Culture: Labor on the Road in Nineteenth-Century East Africa*. Portsmouth, NH: Heinemann.

Rushohora, Nancy Alexander (2015). "An Archaeological Identity of the Majimaji: Towards an Historical Archaeology of Resistance to German Colonisation in Southern Tanzania." PhD Thesis, University of Pretoria.

Rushohora, Nancy. A., & Kurmman. E. (2017). "Looking at Majimaji! A Plea for Historical Photographs in Tanzania." African Studies. 77(1): 87-104, DOI: 10.1080/00020184.2017.1395584.

Shiraz, D. (1984). "Maji Maji: The Tanzanian People's War of National Liberation against German Colonialism, 1904-1907." Sauti ya Kamukunji, 3(1): 10–12.

Unangst, Matthew (2015). "Building the Colonial Border Imaginary: German Colonialism, Race, and Space in East Africa, 1884-1895." Doctoral Thesis. Temple University.

URT (2005). National Strategy for Gender Development. Dar es Salaam: The Ministry of Health, Community Development, Gender, Elderly and Children.

URT (2016). Tanzania Country Gender Profile. Dar es Salaam: The Ministry of Health, Community Development, Gender, Elderly and Children.

Wójtowicz, Beata (2022). "A glimpse at the history of Swahili lexicography. ResearchGate. 413 - 426.

CHAPTER THREE

HEROINES OF MAJIMAJI WAR IN TANZANIA FROM 1905 TO 1907

Dr. Sakina Faru

3.1 Introduction and General Background

3.1.1 Introduction

This chapter on, "Heroines of Majimaji War in Tanzania from 1905 to 1907" brings to light importance of women's participation in the said war at diverse capacities. The presentation is along the following parts: general background; women's participation in wars, theory in recognition of Majimaji war heroines, discussions and concluding remarks.

3.1.2 General Background

Considerably, many scholarly works have been conducted in African historiography concerning scramble for Africa and African colonisation (Dimkpa, 2015). For instance, effects of colonisation, the manner colonisation destabilised as well as caused African underdevelopment were reported by several scholars including Fanon (1961) and Rodney (1973). Additionally, Asiwaju (1985), Dowden (2008) and Wesseling (1996) argued that Europeans gained influence in Africa through colonization and improper border creation. Such position was emphasised by Herbst (2000) who argued that boundaries were greatly a resulting element of the colonial state. Moreover, according to Horowitz (1985), ethnic division of Africa led to desire of one state to annex the territory of another state as well as encouraged beliefs of withdrawal or formal separation from an alliance or federation and nationalism.

In another vein, Africans' hatred to colonialism made them deny such mode of ruling owing much to what colonialism did to Africans (Msellemu, 2012). Colonial regimes exercised land estrangement and imposed taxation as well as forced labour together with other forms of oppression to Africans (*ibid.*). Accordingly, in the fight for their rights, Africans opted to resist against colonialism mirrored through political liberation that aimed at termination of foreign power (*ibid.*).

However, the history of scramble for Africa and subsequently, African colonisation is beyond the scope of this chapter. This chapter is centred on aspects of negative effects of colonialism, secession as well as patriotism that led to resistance wars around the world as well as Africa, in general, and Majimaji war in Tanzania, in particular, thereby depicting heroines of Majimaji War. In so doing, this chapter demonstrates several heroines around the world including Africa, in general and Tanzania's heroines of Majimaji war, in particular.

In comprehending about significance of women's participation in war, essentially during resistance wars against various forms of colonialism, it is important to know that women's partaking during war engulfs a notion entrenched in the discussion around gender (Faasse, 2017). According to Faasse (2017: 16), the following important questions need consideration: in what manner are statuses including roles of women comprehended in the principally masculine environment of warfare? To what degree are women visible in war times? In what manner do women actively participate? Does women's participation substantiate their approved as well as supposed gender roles or do they diverge from the norm at such point? Responses to these questions are provided in subsequent paragraphs.

War as a masculine sphere: Most scholars on war present aspects pertaining to men and they assume that warfare is a masculine sphere and thus, men are said to create wars, make war resolutions, battle wars, make decisions in war, benefit from war, incite war or suffer from war (Shekhawat, 2015). Men are renowned to be violent and active in times of war, while women are said to be passive as well as peace-loving humans in this respect (Coulter *et al.*, 2008). Consequently, people assume the following stance: 'women equal peace and men equal war' (Ala, 2006). Accordingly, the discussions on belief that war is for men together with its associated functional attributes ascribed to men chip in the chief dialogue, which leads to saying like 'fighting men and peaceful women,' implying that one gender fights, whereas the other suffers as well as mourns (Faasse, 2017).

Extent women are viewed in war times: The majority of proponents on women and war assume that women are victims of war or they are unofficial peace makers (Shekhawat, 2015; Faasse, 2017). As a result, women are frequently viewed as more in danger than men owing to sexual or gender-based violence, losses, widowhood, dislocation or disgrace/dishonour (Durnham and Gurd, 2005). Hence, it is imperative to view further that there is unfair treatment or discrimination of women in armed conflicts and then identify that women are not only victims during wartime but also they are essentially people with organization (*ibid.*).

Women partake numerous roles and situations in times of conflict, for instance, they are conciliators, leaders, fighters, supporters or contestants of war (*ibid.*). Moreover, associating women to peace derives from their capability to offer life, while, in the converse, men are perceived as killers (Ala, 2006). However, calling women as inactive humans by design leads to keeping them out by designating a nonstop inferior status in the milieu of armed clash (*ibid.*).

Women's roles in war times: Then another question looms on the manner women are seen by scholars pertaining to their roles in wartimes. Literature on the theme of women and war concentrates by referring to women's unfair treatment or ill-treatment as well as conciliatory capabilities but their responsibility as women fighters and war adherents, to an enormous degree, is disregarded (Darden, 2015). Even though the centre of attention on women as victims and conciliators in conflict is significant, it does not to provide an absolute and sincere portrait of women's diversified responsibilities during war (Faasse, 2017). Those who support or get involved in fighting are ignored and their active responsibilities in war are always seen as supporting fighters, while their active responsibilities in armed conflicts are always masked (Darden, 2015).

Gender Labels on Women and War: People ordinarily, through gender customs, traditionally consider women's involvement in wars as abnormal or aberrant or an alteration (Faasse, 2017). On one hand, it is always a case whereby men are conscripted to join armies during war and then refuse are frequently mocked, imprisoned or even executed for their weakness or short of manliness (*ibid.*). On the other hand, women who go up against female labels in war are regularly considered as abnormal or perverted (*ibid.*). Additionally, there is tendency in asserting that women are unable to take part in fighting and that if they are aggressive, they do so owing to their being maltreated and thus, refute the fact that women may possibly take action as executors (*ibid.*). Such supposition owes to the conviction that women are only caring and peaceable or non-violent humans, incapable to do something aggressively (*ibid.*).

Viewpoints on women's participation to war: There are two polarised views concerning women fighters during war (Faasse, 2017). Firstly, according Maninger (2008), it is argued that, "any form of exclusion of women in the military constitutes an act of discrimination or sexism, the sole objective of which is to irrationally defend a 'man's domain." Such viewpoint is mostly employed by liberal and equality feminists (Faasse, 2017). Exclusion of women from war is alleged to be patriarchal and a lee way to keep out women from decision-making (*ibid.*). Moreover, such viewpoint chiefly makes on constructionism paradigm of gender discussion (Weber, 2006).

Nonetheless, a highly traditionalist standpoint on female fighters denotes to biological as well as sociological distinctions between men and women by contending that women encounter severe restrictions compared to men (Maninger, 2008). Accordingly, such viewpoint associates the essentialist approach to gender owing to the fact that the contention is '… based on fixed physical and psychological differences between men and women' (Weber, 2006). The discussion led proponents to surmise that women are unsuitable for battle or support responsibilities in war due to sociological as well as biological restrictions (Faasse, 2017: 18). Supposed distinctive male features, for instance, aggressiveness, vigour, audacity, resilience, endurance and eagerness to kill as well as encounter danger are argued for reasons that '… the military is a male domain' (*ibid.*: 18). As a result, women are viewed '… as peace-loving, passive, gentle and prudish, which makes them unsuited for combat roles and even jeopardizing the effectiveness of fighting forces' (Carreiras & Kümmel, 2008). Accordingly, with all viewpoints on women who participate in war, they may be marginalized or forgotten and instead of being viewed as fighters, women are labelled as 'camp followers' (Coulter, 2008).

Women's active participation in war: Women's active participation in war includes '… fighting, recruiting, bombing, directing, facilitating, administrating, and spying, to nurturing, caring or being depicted as wives or girlfriends of male combatants…' (Faasse, 2017: 19). Additionally, such females take care of the wounded, they cook, they undertake administrative roles or cleaning and carry out multiple other responsibilities (*ibid.*: 19). Furthermore, women partake in wars/conflicts by taking up arms and perform other chores for fighters, for instance, '… spying, smuggling, killing, recruiting, or being a porter or messenger' (*ibid.*: 19). Even though women are frequently masked in wars/conflict, in fact, they are greatly involved in wars/conflicts at numerous levels (Faasse, 2017). Accordingly, women unceasingly mix together in the masculine sphere of militarization and dispute the conjecture that warfare is inevitably a male sphere (Carreiras & Kümmel, 2008).

3.2 Women's Participation in Liberation Struggles

This section presents women's participation in liberation struggles under two sub-sections. The first sub-section presents selected cases where women participated in wars in African countries. The other sub-section presents materials on women's participation in Majimaji war.

3.2.1 Women's Participation in Wars in Africa

In Africa, women have participated in liberation against colonialism and in current rebel revolts (Coulter *et al.*, 2008). During colonialism in Africa, women took part in a variety of protests against colonial oppression and struggles for independence (Dimkpa, 2015). According to Parpart (1986), African woman proved their courage as political activists during nationalist struggles. Women did so with dedication, eagerness including effectual combined action and as a result, they played an outstanding function in early African nationalist struggles in West, East and Central Africa (*ibid*.). Such struggles were notable in many countries, for instance, Algeria, Kenya, Mozambique, Angola, Guinea-Bissau, Zimbabwe, Namibia, as well as South Africa and they included women fighters, activists and supporters in provision of non-battle services (Kombo, 2012; Coulter *et al.*, 2008).

There were several women's branches in Zambia, under nationalist parties named as the African National Congress (ANC) and later it was renamed the United National Independence Party (UNIP) that staged rural as well as urban protests (Parpart, 1986). There was a women's Brigade that carried out education to aid voter registration and assisted in organisation of funerals in urban areas, mass protests, rallies as well as boycotts (*ibid*.). In Cameroon, women employed a customary practice, known as Anlu that overhauled into a highly arranged association in making the supreme Chire and his executive council powerless (*ibid*.). Moreover, the ruler was deposed from the ruling party, known as Kamerun National Congress (KNC) in the 1959 election and such women assisted to make the Kamerun National Democratic Party (KNDP) into power (*ibid*.).

There were noteworthy feminist as well as anti-colonial protests against British colonialism in Nigeria under the rubric 'Abe Women Riot' (Dimkpa, 2015: 19). The insurgence led by thousands of women in Owerri as well as Calabar Provinces in South-Eastern Nigeria in November and December, 1929 were mainly resistances against enforced high taxes for undertaking businesses in markets (Dimkpa, 2015: 19; Kombo, 2012). In response to such protests, the British killed more than 50 women (Dimkpa, 2015: 19).

In another vein, in Nigeria, particularly in the political domain, market women's support or denial of political candidates was a key feature in political life (Parpart, 1986). From 1920s, there was a women's organisation leader, Oyinkan Morenike Abayomi, who later founded the Nigerian Women's Party (NWP) in 1944 to defended 'women from being cheated by Nigerian men and the government' (*ibid.*: 7). The leader considered women, including well-off, endured suffering from lack of representation in government spheres and thus, she started to remedy such stance (*ibid.*). In the end, the NWP women in Nigeria made Nigerian women maintain to be significant members of later, new nationalist parties (*ibid.*).

Additionally, in Guinea, during independence struggles, women assisted Sekou Toure, who later became the first president after independence, in many avenues (*ibid.*). They assisted him to achieve power through giving money to the nationalist struggle, they provided communication linkages among leaders and they participated in policy decision-making (*ibid.*). Thus, women in Guinea, similar to many West African women, supported '… the nationalist struggle with their economic resources and contacts' (*ibid.*: 8).

The presented women's nationalist struggles in West Africa were not violent. The situation was quite different in southern Africa. Such pattern was true in Portuguese colonies, British colonial rulers and in the then South African apartheid regime whereby women fought in their struggles for independence together with men (Parpart, 1986).

Women were integrated into Zimbabwe liberation war first, in rural communities and second, at the military base camps in neighbouring countries, namely, Mozambique, Botswana and Zambia (Kombo, 2012). In Zimbabwe, women took to arms and fought as guerrillas such that by the end of the war, women accounted for almost a quarter out of 30,000 combatants in the Patriotic Front organisation (Parpart, 1986: 8). It was approximated that women in the military camps encompassed almost a quarter or one-third of volunteers of the Zimbabwean liberation armies (Kombo, 2012).

During the apartheid regime in South Africa, women of all backgrounds in terms of race and ethnicity resisted against apartheid and racial injustice (*ibid*: 8). For instance, in 1950s, the Bantu Women's League of the African National Congress (ANC) were at the forefront in the fight against racial prejudice (*ibid.*). Notable women leaders, as heroines, namely, Maxeke offered distinguished leadership on women's and black people's matters and later on, the late Winnie Mandela, during her lifetime, provided undaunted leadership to such cause (*ibid.*).

According to Katto (2020), after formation of Frente de Libertacão de Mocambique (FRELIMO) in 1962, the *Liga Feminina Mocambicana* (the League of Mozambican Women, LIFEMO) was created. Even though some were already conscripted by FRELIMO in 1965, their official integration into the guerrilla army took place alongside formation of FRELIMO's Destacamento Feminino (DF, female detachment) in 1967 (*ibid.*). Such recruits, composed of girls and young women as well as received political and military training (Katto, 2020; Coulter *et al.*, 2008). The DF (for girls and young women) took part in armed fighting, collected intelligence information as well as rallied civilian support (Coulter *et al.*, 2008).

Of special note is that shortly after Mozambique attained independence in 1975, there ensued civil war from 1976 to 1992 between the rebel group, Resistencia Nacional de Mocambique (RE NAMO) and government forces under FRELIMO (Coulter *et al.*, 2008). Such conflict necessited involvement of young women and girls in both fighting forces (*ibid.*). The female fighters in FRELIMO and RENAMO carried out various responsibilities that included fighters, trainers of new recruits, "... intelligence officers, spies, recruiters, medics, first aid technicians, weapons experts, forced and domestic labourers, and captive 'wives' of male fighters" (*ibid.*: 11).

In East Africa, Kenya presents a vivid example of women fighters. In Kenya, a feminist anti-colonial insurgence was staged under the name, Mau Mau resistance whereby several Wakikuyu women took direct confrontation with British colonial power (Dimkpa, 2015). Such women had division of tasks that included information gathering for Mau Mau fighters, arms smuggling and provision of food as well as medicine to men combatants in the forests (Dimkpa, 2015; Kombo, 2012).

According to Msellemu (2012: 151), Mau Mau is likely a contraction for Kiswahili words, *Mzungu Aende Ulaya Mwafrika Apate Uhuru*, translated in English as Let the white man go back to Europe so that Africans can get Independence. Nonetheless, Wakikuyu did not ascribe to the term Mau Mau movement and instead, they named it in several phrases in Kikuyu dialect as *Muingi,* the movement in English, '*Muingithania,* The Unifier in English and '*Muma wa Uigano,*' The Oath of Unity' (*ibid.*).

Moreover, Mau Mau revolt happened due to increased economic tension together with lack of peaceful political situation in Kenya highlands (Msellemu, 2012; Kombo, 2012). In their pursuit, from 1942 to 1943, Wakikuyu introduced ritual oath taking that was administered to all groups of people, young men, women and children in ensuring shared team spirit or cohesion (Msellemu, 2012). Some women were leaders during oath ceremonies whereby they recruited new members, hosted the oath rituals and in fact, administered the oaths (Kombo, 2012). It is presumed that a quarter of all Wakikuyu women dynamically supported the colonial resistance and as already presented, they were involved in various responsibilities in the Mau Mau as oath administrators, fighters, coordinators of weapons acquiring from enemy soldiers, arbitrators and procurers of food including other supplies for forest combatants (*ibid.*).

However, the colonial rule dealt with such Mau Mau women. Mau Mau women members were forced to give up all loyalty to the Mau Mau (Kombo, 2012). Some figures demonstrate the counts of Mau Mau women imprisoned by the British colonial regime (*ibid.*). The numbers show an increment over the year during their imprisonment from 347 in 1952 to 13, 265 in 1955 as the Mau Mau war continued (*ibid.*: 45).

3.2.2   Women's Participation in Majimaji War

This part presents on women's participation in Majimaji War. It provides a brief overview on the war itself and concentrates on dealing with women's partaking in the said war. Details of the war in all of its dimensions are beyond the scope of this chapter.

3.2.2.1   Brief Overview of Majimaji War

Majimaji uprising first broke out in Lindi and Kilwa districts of Lindi region that involved Wangindo communities among the first to revolt against German oppression (Greiner, 2022). The war was waged against the colonial state's representatives and as a consequence, it involved damage to the physical landscape, for instance, they sabotaged kilometre marker stones along the constructed Kilwa road that formerly engrossed people's forced labour (*ibid.*). In August, 1907 owing to gradual suppression, the war ended (*ibid.*).

Furthermore, causes of Majimaji war were diverse and proponents like Gwassa (1973: 10) and Rushohora (2015: 119) cautioned that no single cause can elucidate '… the war to the fullest and the war was not spontaneous." Besides, motives to partake in the said war differed from one region to another (Sunseri, 2010: 141; Rushohora, 2015: 202). In general, causes of Majimaji war included forced cotton cultivation together with rubber extraction, heavy taxation, and compulsory labour as well as harassment in road construction (Rushohora, 2015).

In terms of its geographic scope, the fierce resistance against German rule went off with varying intensity across most parts of the country (Greiner, 2022; De Juan, 2016; Rushohora, 2015). As already reported, Lindi and Kilwa districts were areas where the resistance first took place in the country (Greiner, 2022). In mid-1905, the Majimaji War broke out in southern Tanzania, from where it spread over large parts of the country (*ibid.*).

The war spread to other parts of the country organised as well as spearheaded by both men and women warriors in fighting against Germans (Shiraz, 1984; Rushohora & Kurmann, 2017; Gregory, 2020). The fighters were drawn from about 20 ethnic groups that included the following: Wamatumbi, Wangindo, Wapogoro, Wamwera, Wayao and Wangoni (Rushohora, 20015). Moreover, Majimaji war had leaders, namely, Ndimi Omcheka, Ngurumbale Mandai and Mtemangani of Kilwa, Kinjekitile Ngwale of Ngarambe-Rufiji, Chief Chabruma, and Nduna of Songea against German colonial rule (Rushohora, 20015; Gregory, 2020). Exceptionally, ethnic groups in the southern areas of the country had many other forms of resistances, for instance, Wapogoro in 1898, Wanyakyusa in 1989 and Wamatengo in 1902 (Rushohora, 2015: 43).

The southern part of the country was the bigger starting place of active Majimaji war than other parts (Rushohora, 2015: 43). For instance, in 1890, the Wayao Chief, Chief Machemba, resisted against Germans led by Commander Herman von Wissmann and upon the Chief's defeat, he fled to Mozambique (Iliffe, 1979 cited in Rushohora, 2015: 43). Additionally, Majimaji war outbreak in 1905 was one of the furthermost challenges that were strongly raised by Chief Mkwawa of Uhehe in Iringa who was defeated by Germans in 1894, but before in 1891, his army killed the German Commander, Zelewski and almost wiped out soldiers (Iliffe, 1979; Rushohora, 2015: 43). However, in 1898, to evade Germans' arrest and execution, Chief Mkwawa committed suicide (Iliffe, 1979: 108; Rushohora, 2015: 43).

Moreover, any war or conflict has its price or consequences and a few are presented. Thus, in the world, many-sided historical tremors, evident through wars/conflicts, for example, Majimaji war, not only had numerous causes but also it had many consequences (Koponen, 2010: 23). Accordingly, Majimaji war had the following consequences: devastation and depopulation; internal changes; changes from extractive to developmental colonialism; and development as well as neglect.

Importantly, consequences denote to what historians agree to the notion that people of southern Tanzania started Majimaji war who targeted the German authority (Rushohora, 2015: 193) and consequently, Majimaji war should be well thought-out destructive and genocidal (Faru, 2023). "However, the counter-charge of genocide on the part of Majimaji fighters cannot be sustained, as there is no incidence where genocide may occur as self-defence" (Rushohora, 2015: 193). According to Rushohora (2015: 193), "The civilian population was systematically targeted: entire villages, fields and granaries were burnt and hunger was used as a weapon to bring the guerrilla fighters to their knees."

Notably, "The German troops used scorched earth policy (Larson, 2010: 110), gendercide (killing of women), genocidal hunger, extermination and mass killings, which were explicitly prohibited under the law of armed conflict that was applicable at the time and which the German imperial troops and their commanders chose to ignore" (Rushohora, 2015: 194). In addition, in 1906, almost one hundred Wangoni elders were executed so as to eliminate the complete military and political elites (Rushohora, 2015: 194). Moreover, Germans carried out military missions and killed traditional healers (Monson, 2010: 36-37).

German soldiers beheaded African chiefs and took their skulls to German on the alleged reason that they carried out treasonable offenses and some were hanged (LeGall, 2020). Scientists measured and compared human remains from all over the world and such "… studies fuelled discourse on biological determinism and Social Darwinist assumptions on race. In the twentieth century, such theories were then politically instrumentalised for oppressive policies such as apartheid or the infamous Nuremberg laws" (*ibid.*: 9). It can be contended that such acts depict "…center of evidence of the colonial crime scene" (*ibid.*: 9).

3.2.2.2 Women's Partaking in Majimaji War

Numerous women participated in Majimaji War at varying dimensions or degrees in the battle field and elsewhere within war areas. However, as Rushohora (2015: 207) notes, very little attention was devoted to Majimaji war heroines. One of Majimaji war women participants, Nkomanile, was a leader in her area of jurisdiction (*ibid.*). Although Nkomanile, who was one of sub-chiefs in Ungoni, is widely discussed, the debate is limited to initiation of recruits into the war in the south western regions through Omari Kinjala (Iliffe, 1967: 173; Mapunda, 2010: 227-228; Rushohora, 2015: 209). There is a gap concerning other aspects of Nkomanile "… including Kitanda as a gendered site, the burial of this female heroine with other males in the mass grave, and an opposition to the common emphasis on both physical and emotional differences between men and women, associating men with strength, aggression and violence and women with their opposites" (Rushohora, 2015: 205).

Kitanda was the area where the female sub-chief Nkomanile ruled and it was the gate through which magic water (*maji* in Kiswahili used with other ingredients as the medicine to war fighters, which the war's name assumes) from Kinjekitile passed to Wangoni and later Upangwa as well as Ubena who too participated in Majimaji war (Rushohora, 2015: 205). She was the only female sub-chief who participated in Majimaji war and was buried in a mass grave (*ibid.*). She was the only woman who was sentenced to death by the Germans (*ibid.*).

Additionally, all the way along the Majimaji war, women were involved in different contexts (*ibid.*: 211). According to Rushohora (2015: 211, 212),

> "… among the Matumbi of Nandete, Jumbe Mtemangani (junior German local representative) sent a letter to his superior at Kibata through his wife Namchanjama. This was after all his immediate officers, including Mtemangani himself refused to take the letter in fear of the reaction. Namchanjama was to report to the Akida (senior German local representative) Seif bin Amri at Kibata German administrative offices. Namchanjama was willing to take the letter and delivered the message. She was killed at Imbiliya hill upon her return to Nandete in a fierce battle between the German representatives at Kibata and Matumbi warriors.

Namchanjama was among the first people who died in the Majimaji war."

Even though many women are not reported for their participation in Majimaji war, they were involved in the war and their roles were varied. Accordingly, some were non-combatants, for instance, "… women are as much a factor as armies, formal or informal" (Rushohora, 2015: 212). Important to note is that the *maji*, water in English as the war medicine, was managed by women who were considerable as well as included elements in ritual activities and in war (Monson, 2010: 37). While men used war medicines to guarantee accuracy of firearms, women took medicines to reinforce them against hardship of flight into woodland hiding places and preserve them from confinement by enemies (Rushohora, 2015: 212). In addition, women were used as spies and accordingly, colonial troops detained women as hostages so as "… to establish whether they were Majimaji supporters or loyalists" (Rushohora, 2015: 212). The technique intended to force surrender by preventing supplies reaching the warriors but acknowledged the important role played by women during warfare (*ibid.*).

3.3   Discussions

The discussion is anchored on two salient parts. The first part presents perception of wartime statuses in gender relations, while the second part is on women's participation in Majimaji War as Unsung Majimaji war heroines.

3.3.1   Perception of wartime statuses in gender relations

It can be deduced that responsibilities and statuses of women fighters varied between different conflicts and fighting forces (Coulter *et al.*, 2008). For instance, in wars like those in Ethiopia, Eritira and Mozambique, women's partaking was considered to be strengthening general aim of liberation and accordingly, women got higher rank positions (*ibid.*). In later wars, for instance, wars in Sierra Leone, Liberia, Uganda and the civil war in Mozambique between the ruling party FRELIMO and resistant faction, RENAMO, particular female fighters were in positions of power, while some had more agency than before war broke (*ibid.*). Nonetheless, women's general positions were low because many were kidnapped, forced to labour and above all, they were abused (*ibid.*). Besides, in some cases, even those who had high statuses during war, they were unnecessarily maintained, in practice, after the war (*ibid.*).

There are other benefits realised by women in later generations as well as later times of conflicts and/or struggles against oppression and struggles for independence in Africa. For instance, currently, in Kenya, a younger generation of Kenyan women envision Mau Mau experience as a positive contribution of women to national liberation (Kombo, 2012). They are motivated to presume decision-making responsibilities in political and economical spheres (*ibid.*). Principally in rural communities, tribute is paid to Mau Mau women in songs and they continue to be an encouragement to village women as well as the urban poor (*ibid.*). Thus, formation of women's cooperatives, self-help clusters and economic ventures are due to inspiration from the Mau Mau women of the previous era (*ibid.*). Such organisations of several developmental associations depict statuses owing to skills women learned in organizing in forest war and in the non-fighting responsibilities during the Mau Mau war were put to organizing numerous developmental associations (*ibid.*).

In Tanzania, Majimaji war became an inspiration to many people after it was renamed from a rebellion to a war and recognised to be an inspiration to national liberation struggles for independence. The war inspired and still inspires many people including women, particularly in politics. For instance, from its inception in its peaceful independence struggles, the ruling party, Tanganyika African National Union (TANU) later on reconstituted as well as renamed as Chama cha Mapinduzi (CCM) honour such motivation to all people in the country. For women, the political party established a women's wing for political empowerment, Umoja wa Wanawake Tanzania (UWT, a women's union of Tanzanian women). There are women leaders in politics as well as ruling and non-ruling political parties from grassroots level to national levels. On part of the government, many women are in government positions including parliamentarians. Besides, the government created a special Ministry dealing with Gender.

3.3.2 Women's Participation in Majimaji War: The Unsung Majimaji war heroines

It is pertinent to assert that women's participations in Majimaji war at varying capacities in their responsibilities are masked. Little is provided concerning their noble participation to such cause of liberation struggle against colonialism. Some were leaders and some were executed. Yet, amidst such statuses and their roles they played, they are not eulogised. Given their participation and their dignified role in Majimaji war, it is safe to call them **unsung Majimaji heroines**.

Such assertion is arrived at using Afriocentricity as a pertinent analytical lens and thus, position germane scholastic undertakings that have to untie or unmask many aspects in an African-centred perspective. Accordingly, studies must be carried out on women as agents of war including their leaders such as Nkomanile and should be widened to the extent of pinpointing where and how gender is included in material discourse thereby investigate outcomes of its presence (see also, Rushohora, 2015: 205; Faru, 2023). Kitanda was the beginning of Ngoni Mchope chiefdom in the proximity of the Ungindo (*ibid.*). Nkomanile was renowned for having ruled Kitanda with generosity and intelligent leadership (Mapunda, 2010: 228). According to Rushohora (2015: 201, 210), Nkomanile was convinced of the power of *maji* and passed information to her superiors who also subscribed to the cause of war.

Nkomanile participated in Majimaji war, but sadly she was persecuted and sentenced to death like other leaders as well as warriors of Ungoni (*ibid.*: 210). Another woman to be considered too as a heroine, with leadership position, was Namabengo but her stance in begging for clemency did not lead to her being persecuted by Germans (*ibid.*). She persuaded the Germans that she did not join the war though it was probably not true and thus, the Germans spared her life (*ibid.*).

3.4 Concluding Remarks

Presented materials in this chapter lead to conclusion due to the fact that women were involved in Majimaji war at varying dimensions or capacities. They are unsung **Majimaji war heroines**. According to Rushohora (2015: 207), very little attention was devoted to Majimaji war heroines and although Nkomanile, who was one of sub-chiefs in Ungoni, is widely discussed, the discussion is confined to initiation of recruits into the war in the south western regions of Tanzania. Women's participation and role in Majimaji war were diverse and "… women are as much a factor as armies, formal or informal" (Rushohora, 2015: 212). Recall, *maji*, the war medicine that led to assumption of the name for the war (Majimaji), was managed by women who were considerable as well as included elements in ritual activities and in war (Monson, 2010: 37). While men used war medicines to guarantee precision of firearms, women took medicines to strengthen them against adversity of flight into woodland hiding places and protected them from arrest by enemies (Rushohora, 2015: 212). In another avenue, women were used as spies (Rushohora, 2015: 212). Therefore, as a way to curb women's participation in the war, colonial troops detained women as hostages so as "… to establish whether they were Majimaji supporters or loyalists" (*ibid.*: 212). The path way intended to force surrender by preventing supplies reaching the warrior groups but it must be acknowledged that women had the important role they played during Majimaji warfare (Rushohora, 2015). Women took active participation in Majimaji war at diverse capacities and even though they are reported to have taken part in the war, they are not accorded the rightful stances. Therefore, it is arguably obvious that although not eulogised, they are unsung Majimaji war heroines.

References

Ala, J. (2006). "Enriching the critical discourse of feminist studies in international relations: New discussions of the roles of women in conflict, peace making and Government." *Politikon: South Africa Journal of Political Studies* 33(2): 239-249.

Asiwaju, A. (1985). "The Conceptual Framework," in Partitioned Africans, pp. 1—18. New York: St. Martin Press.

Carreiras, H. and Kümmel, G. (2008). Off Limits: The Cults of the Body and Social Homogeneity as Discoursive Weapons Targeting Gender Integration in the Military. In H. Carreiras, & G. Kümmel eds. *Women in the Military and in Armed Conflict,* pp. 29-47). VS Verlag für Sozialwissenschafte.

Coulter, C. (2008). "Female fighters in the Sierra Leone war: challenging the assumptions?" Feminist Review 88(1): 54-73.

Coulter, C., Persson, M., & Utas, M. (2008). *Young female fighters in African wars: Conflict and Its Consequences.* Stockholm: Nordiska Afrikainstitutet.

Darden, J. (2015). "Assessing the significance of women in combat roles." International Journal 70(3): 454 - 462.

De Juan, A. (2016). "Extraction and Violent Resistance in the Early Phases of State Building: Quantitative Evidence From the 'Maji Maji' Rebellion, 1905-1907." *Comparative political studies* 49(3): 291-323. https:// doi.org/10.1177/0010414015617962.

Dimkpa, Princewill (2015). Colonialism, Independence and Underdevelopment in Africa: The Pre-eminence and Blame Game. M. A. Dissertation in African Studies, University of Dalarna.

Dowden, R. (2008). *Africa: Altered States, Ordinary Miracles*. London: Portobello Books Limited.

Durnham, H., and Gurd, T. (2005). *Listening to the Silences: Women and War*. Leiden: Martinus Nijhoff Publishers.

Faasse, Else Lotte (2017). "Female Participants in Armed Conflict: The Case of Sierra Leone." Thesis in Bachelor of Science in International Development Studies, Wageningen University and Research Centre (WUR).

Fanon, Frantz (1961). *The Wretched of the Earth*. London: Penguin Books.

Faru, Sakina (2023). "In memory of genocide against members of Majimaji Movement in Tanzania from 1905 to 1907." Paper presented to the International Week (2023) at Hochschule Bielefeld - University of Applied Sciences and Arts (HSBI), Germany.

Gregory, Athanasy (2020). "The Role of Women in Maji Maji War from 1905 to 1907 in Matumbiland, Ngindo and Ngoniland War Zones, Tanzania." East African Journal of Education and Social Sciences. 1(3): 52-59. DOI: https://doi.org/10.46606/eajess2020v01i03.0042 URL: http://eajess.ac.tz

Greiner, Andreas (2022). "Colonial Schemes and African Realities: Vernacular Infrastructure and the Limits of Road Building in German East Africa." The Journal of African History 63(3): 328–347 doi:10.1017/S0021853722000500.

Gwassa, G.C.K. (1973). "The Outbreak and Development of the Maji Maji War, 1905-1907." Ph.D. Thesis, University of Dar es Salaam.

Herbst, J. (2000). *States and Power in Africa*. Princeton: Princeton University Press.

Iliffe, J. (1969). "Tanzania Under German and British Rule." in Zamani: A Survey of East African History, ed. B. A. Ogot and J. A. Kieran, pp. 2 90-301. Nairobi: East African Publishing House.

Katto, Jonna (2020). *Women's Lived Landscapes of War and Liberation in Mozambique: Bodily Memory and the Gendered Aesthetics of Belonging*. New York: Routledge.

Kombo, E. E. (2012). "Women in National Liberation Wars in the Settler Colonies of Kenya and Zimbabwe: Pathways to Political Empowerment." M.A. dissertation, Women's Studies, University of York.

Koponen, J. (2010). "Maji Maji in the Making of the South." *Tanzania Zamani: A Journal of History Research and Writing.* 7(1): 1-58. http://hdl.handle.net/10138/252452

LeGall, Yann (2020). "Songea Mbano and the 'halfway dead' of the Majimaji War (1905–7) in memory and theatre." *Human Remains and Violence.* 6(2): 4–22. http://dx.doi.org/10.7227/HRV.6.2.

Luna K.C. and Gemma Van Der Haar (2019). "Living Maoist gender ideology: experiences of women ex-combatants in Nepal." *International Feminist Journal of Politics*, 21(3): 434-453, DOI: 10.1080/14616742.2018.1521296

Maninger, S. (2008). "Women in combat: Reconsidering the case against the deployment of women in combat-support and combat units." In H. Carreiras and G. Kümmel eds. *Women in the Military and in Armed Conflict,* pp. 9-27. Wiesbaden: VS Verlag für Sozialwissenschaften/GWV Fachverlage GmbH.

Mapunda, B. B. (2010). "Re-examining the Maji Maji War in Ungoni with a Blend of Archaeology and Oral History." In eds. J. Giblin and J. Manson, *Maji Maji: Lifting the Fog of War.* pp. 220-238. Leiden, Boston: Brill.

Monson, J. (2010). War of Words: The narrative efficacy of medicine in the Maji Maji War. In eds. Giblin, J. and Monson, J. *Maji Maji Lifting the Fog of War.* Pp. 33 – 69. Leiden, Boston: Brill.

Msellemu, Sengulo Albert (2012). "Common Motives of Africa's Anti-colonial Resistance in 1890–1960." Social Evolution & History, 12(2): 143 – 155.

Parpart, Jane L. (1986). "Women and the State in Africa." Department of History, Dalhousie University Halifax, Canada Working Paper Number 117: 1-27.

Rodney, Walter (1973). *How Europe Underdeveloped Africa.* Dar es Salaam: Tanzania Publishing House.

Rushohora, Nancy Alexander (2015). "An Archaeological Identity of the Majimaji: Towards an Historical Archaeology of Resistance to German Colonisation in Southern Tanzania." PhD Thesis, University of Pretoria.

Rushohora, Nancy. A. & Kurmman. E. (2017). "Looking at Majimaji! A Plea for Historical Photographs in Tanzania." *African Studies*. 77(1): 87-104, DOI: 10.1080/00020184.2017.1395584.

Shekhawat, S. (2015). *Female Combatants in Conflict and Peace: Challenging Gender in Violence and Post-Conflict Reintegration.* New York: Springer.

Shiraz, D. (1984). "Maji Maji: The Tanzanian People's War of National Liberation against German Colonialism, 1904-1907." Sauti ya Kamukunji, 3(1): 10–12.

Sunseri, T. (2010). "The War of the Hunters: Maji Maji and the Decline of the Ivory Trade." in Maji Maji Lifting the Fog of War, ed. J. Giblin and J. Monson, pp. 117-148. Brill, Boston

Weber, A. (2006). Feminist peace and conflict theory. *Encyclopaedia on Peace and Conflict Theory*, 2-13.

Wesseling, H. L. (1996). *Divide and Rule: The Partition of Africa, 1880-1914.* Amsterdam: Praeger.

CHAPTER FOUR

QUESTIONS OF REPATRIATION OF HUMAN REMAINS, ANIMAL REMAINS, PLANT REMAINS AND CULTURAL OBJECTS FROM TANZANIA IN THE GERMAN COLONIAL PERIOD

By Charles Saanane

4.0 Introduction

This chapter focuses on recovered/discovered human remains, animal remains, plant remains and cultural materials that were collected, transported and stored in Germany as a result of German colonial rule. It starts with a brief description on drivers of exploration and scientific expeditions around the world. Other aspects include collected, transported and stored materials in Germany. Also, the chapter includes an overview on international measures undertaken and currently observed pertaining to repatriation of the said materials, discussion on materials that have been returned to Tanzania together with looming questions concerning the materials and future prospects to that end.

4.1 Drivers of exploration and scientific expeditions around the world

Geographical discoveries as well as trades by Europeans, contacts with people and colonization insightfully changed non-European societies around the world (Maughan, n.d.). European explorers ushered in infiltration of traders together with institution of Christian missions (*ibid.*). Thus, explorers, merchants as well as missionaries were critical to building of European commercial and cultural exchange (*ibid.*). It is reckoned further that beginning of the sixteenth century, Europeans were increasingly interested in the other parts of the world and accordingly, they were inspired by desire for riches, reputation/honour, development of Christianity, power and charity (*ibid.*).

Knowledge on natural history and geography changed in the eighteenth century through systematic analysis of nearly all reachable areas of the earth (Iliffe, 2003). As a result, the kind of expeditions that were based on scientific objectives went through quick advancements (*ibid.*). Moreover, scientific exploration together with imperial knowledge systems was devised to institute geographical knowledge in serving royal desires (Maughan, n.d.). They instituted programmes to assemble economic along with planned lists of geographical, botanical as well as anthropological pieces of information and they were sponsored by learned societies, for example, Royal Society in London (*ibid.*). The Royal Society in London pushed for exploration of South Pacific, the Arctic and Africa (*ibid.*). Additionally, from the eighteenth century, exploration in Africa involved numerous German, French and British parties (*ibid.*).

In the seventeenth century, there were,

> "Ground-breaking examples of which were sponsored by the Académie Royale des Sciences in the seventeenth century to procure information useful for navigation. Under the protection of Colbert and Louis XIV, the Académie actively promoted three voyages … that were undertaken with the explicit intention of testing the feasibility of using clocks or Jupiter's satellites to determine longitude, the perennial problem of the sailor. While cartography prospered in Paris through the work of Gian Domenico Cassini and Jean Picard, Jean Richer travelled to Cayenne … and made measurements on a pendulum that were used by Newton in his *Principia Mathematica* of 1687 to demonstrate that the earth was flattened at the poles. The Royal Society of London published advice in the early numbers of the *Philosophical Transactions* for sailors and gentlemen travellers to make observations in ethnography and natural history and to report back to both the Society and the Admiralty. This influenced the Narborough expedition … which was

supposed to report in detail on the coastlines, minerals, and flora and fauna of the South Pacific, although strategically the affair was disappointing" (Iliffe, 2003: 621).

Later on in the nineteenth century, scholastic societies and private associations were guarantors to explorations (Lawrence, 2015). As a result, botanical gardens and horticultural societies paid for plant collectors to join already extant expeditions (*ibid.*). In another vein, rich persons sponsored their employees to travel so as to collect samples for them (*ibid.*).

Outstandingly, from the initial times, travelling around the world was considered the main ingredient in economic improvement, directly linked with naval as well as military operations and trade (Lawrence, 2015; Labadie (2021). Initial explorations were always backed up by governments keen for territorial expansion or by private trading companies, for example, the Dutch East India Company that "… traded in spices, commercial goods, curiosities and medicinal substances" (Lawrence, 2015). Thus, Britain, the continental European countries, the United States of America and Russia wanted to expand their powers overseas (Lawrence, 2015; Iliffe, 2003). On the other hand, scientific and medical pieces of information availed to Europe were greatly valued (Lawrence, 2015).

Just before the end of the nineteenth century, big science emerged, international scientific consolidation ensued and large-scale scientific research voyages were carried out (*ibid.*). As a result, expeditions provided considerable "… insight into the social structure and theory-base of nineteenth-century science and natural history" (*ibid.*). Thus, science fast became an internationalised quest such that major urban centres, for example, Berlin, London and Paris became vital for processing results from such expeditions (*ibid.*). Moreover, old royal notion of "…'centre and periphery,'" with the former "… being the place where information was converted into scientific 'facts,' suited scholars in developed countries very well and contributed materially to the specialisation of their disciplines" (*ibid.*).

So, for Tanzania, there is history of foreign expeditions that were carried out. Anthropological research and thus, collection of material objects started from the beginning of arrival of early missionaries as well as explorers in the mid-nineteenth century (Chami *et al.*, 2023). It was the initial time Europeans began to involve with Tanzanian communities and took or received gifts from traditional elders or leaders along with materials considered by contemporary societies as valuable cultural heritage (Perras,

2004; Kayombo, 2005). Accordingly, from the early 1880s to 1914, many missions were conducted by Germans to explore and survey mainland Tanzania's people and resources (*op. cit.*).

4.2 Collected Human Remains, Animal Remains, Plant Remains and Cultural Objects from Tanzania during German Rule

It has to be accredited that German scientists pioneered scientific research endeavours in many disciplines, including geology, geography, anthropology and many others in Tanzania. They collected human remains from extant species and also, they collected proto-human species (fossils) that are extinct that mostly, owing to scientific and technical ability, they shipped them to Germany.

4.2.1 Collected Human Remains from Tanzania during German Rule

4.2.1.1 Collected human remains from contemporary people during Germany Colonial rule

Many non-European human remains were collected around the world and sent to Germany. Almost 10,000 non-European human remains were kept in Berlin alone until after World War II (Stoecker and Winkelmann 2018; Winkelmann, 2020). According to Winkelmann (2020), such number may have been close to 20,000 for Germany in total. Particularly, a number of human remains were acquired prior to formal beginning of German colonialism in 1884, nevertheless, the majority of repatriated remains were those obtained during the German Empire [(1871-1918) *ibid.*].

Chief Mkwawa's resistance to German rule: Historical records unveil that Chief Mwanamtwa Mkwawa (1855-1898) was the dominant leader of Wahehe community (in Uhehe kingdom) in the currently known region, Iringa (Willoughby *et al.*, 2019). Chief Mkwawa stalwartly resisted German colonial infiltration into the Southern Highlands of what was Tanganyika, presently known as mainland Tanzania (Iliffe, 1979: 57; Willoughby *et al.*, 2019). In general, he is referred to as the most distinguished chief of the Uhehe kingdom such that in the nineteenth century, his kingdom became the overruling power in Iringa (Iliffe, 1979: 57). He united as well as connected

Wahehe and conquered small kinship-based chiefdoms in the region, which efficiently turned Uhehe kingdom into a tough militarized political entity (Crema, 2004). Besides, it was mandatory for every adult male to be a combatant (Iliffe, 1979: 57).

Wahehe had numerous victories against Germans before their defeat and it is reported that on the night of 17th and 18th August 1891, Wahehe soldiers ambushed and defeated the Germans in vicinities of Lugalo, about 27 kilometres east of Iringa town (Redmayne, 1968; Crema, 2004). In the battle, Wahehe soldiers killed more than 300 of German troops together with their commander, Emil von Zelewski (Willoughby et al., 2019; Monson, 2000; Crema, 2004). According to Muso (2011), Wahehe's victory at Lugalo, motivated Mkwawa's armed forces such that at Kilosa, in Morogoro region, they carried out an effective surprise attack and defeated the Germans. The battle at Kilosa reinstated German self-assurance such that on 28th October, 1894, they directly attacked Mkwawa's fortified capital at Kalenga, west of Iringa town, and demolished Kalenga thereby forced Chief Mkwawa to escape to Mlambalasi village, where he lived at or in the main rock shelter (Redmayne, 1968; Musso, 2011). Armed with military tactics, Mkwawa employed guerrilla fighting that led to periodic fights between his army and the Germans (*ibid.*). The fight ensued for four years up to 1898 when Mkwawa shot himself instead of surrendering to Germans (Redmayne, 1968; Crema 2004).

One of Mkwawa's servants informed Germans regarding Chief Mkwawa's death and later, German soldiers commanded by Sign Merk confirmed the report physically at Mlambalasi (Redmayne, 1970). Upon finding Mkwawa's dead body, Sign Merk shot the remains in the head to ensure that the Chief was dead (*ibid.*). Several items including "… various medicines, a half-filled cartridge belt, a carbine rifle and 117 cartridges" were found beside Mkwawa's dead body (Iliffe, 1979: 116).

After preparations to get the skull, it was displayed as a trophy at Prince's residence, a German regional leader in Iringa (Willoughby et al., 2019). Later on, the Prince sent the skull to Bremen Anthropological Museum in Germany and it remained until the 1950s when it was returned to Tanzania during British rule (Willoughby et al., 2019).

Moreover, Majimaji War: Majimaji war that occurred between 1905 and 1907 in southern Tanzania was among resistances against German colonial rule (Rushohora, 2019, 2015). There were atrocities that included killings during the war. Nonetheless, there is no clear testimony as to whether or not Chiefs who led Majimaji war and their warriors' body parts (skeletal materials – skulls or post-cranial materials) were separated from their bodies and then sent to Germany. Rushohora's (2015) study unveils that Chief Songea Mbano's family members believe that their grandfather's body was be-headed. They claim that his head was sent to Germany (*ibid.*). There is a mass grave that includes the grave of Chief Songea Mbano together with Majimaji warriors' graves at Songea Majimaji War Memorial Museum (*ibid.*). Besides, there are no written sources that confirm such claims by Chief Songea Mbano's family members (*ibid.*) and if so, it implies that the grave of Chief Songea Mbano has his skeletal remains with no skull – thus, the gave has post-cranial remains.

According to Mnyaka Sururu Mboro's account, like elsewhere in mainland Tanzania (then Tanganyika), Germans forcibly wanted to install their regime in Kilimanjaro. But they faced fierce resistance from Wachagga under their leader, namely, Mangi Meli (in Kichagga and Chief in English) and through confrontation they killed him along with others (Le Gall, 2019). Following such incident there was be-heading of victims that included Mangi Meli (*ibid.*). It is believed that their skulls were sent to Germany and they are yet to be repatriated to Tanzania (*ibid.*). Mr. Mnyaka Sururu Mboro is grandson of Mangi Meli and he lives in Germany working with a Non-Governmental Organisation (NGO) called, *Berlin Postkolonial e.V.* (*ibid.*). He works for "… recognition of German colonial history in the capital and elsewhere. … also strongly focuses on the repatriation of human remains looted in colonized countries like Tanzania and brought to Europe and Germany for racist research" (*ibid.*).

In 1910, the Geographical Society (Geographische Gesellschaft) in Hamburg, Germany commissioned the Hamburg geographer Erich Obst with a research trip to German East Africa (Chami *et al.*, 2023. Besides, the trip was supported by the German Colonial Office (Reichskolonialamt) and endowed with some of the scientific equipment on loan and afterwards paid production costs for route surveys and maps (*ibid.*). He carried out archaeological excavations in Isanzu area, Singida region (*ibid.*).

> "Obst sent all the excavated ancestral remains from the expedition to the Geographische Gesellschaft in Hamburg, which then handed them over to the Hamburg Museum für Völkerkunde. There, the sixty-eight skulls and skeletons including twenty-two from Isanzu ethnic group were added to the museum's anthropological collection and inventoried

in 1912 (MARKK archive, 786). In the 1950s and 1960s, the contents of the Anthropological Collection of the Museum für Völkerkunde Hamburg (today MARKK, Museum am Rothenbaum. Kulturen und Künste der Welt) were transferred to the Anatomical Institute of the University of Göttingen, thus dissolving the Anthropological Department of the Hamburg Museum in the late 1950s. At the University of Göttingen, the Anthropological Collection moved around 1972 to the newly founded Anthropological Institute where the collection is still curated today" (*ibid.*: 162).

Chami and colleagues' (2023) study uncovered through their respondents who mentioned the local people's leader in Isanzu area, Chief Kitentemi was arrested by Germans. It was presumed that he was hung and his skull was taken to Germany (*ibid.*). He was taken away by the Germans, never to return to Isanzu again (*ibid.*: 166). However, respondents thought that some other human remains, presumably like their chief, were hung by Germans and buried them near their fort but took away their skulls to Germany (*ibid.*).

4.2.1.2 Collected proto-human remains from Tanzania during Germany colonial rule

Owing to discovery of human skeletal remains by a German Physician at Olduvai Gorge in Arusha region northern Tanzania, in 1911, Dr. Wilhelm Kattwinkel and later in 1913, a German Geologist, Hanz Reck carried out scientific investigation in the area and recovered proto-human skeletal remains code named Olduvai Hominid I [(OH 1) Matu *et al.*, 2017]. It is the first fossil to be discovered and the only *Homo sapiens* recovered at the site (*ibid.*). The specimen was shipped to Germany and housed at Bavarian State Collection for Anthropology and Palaeoanatomy of Munich [(Germany) *ibid.*].

Subsequent research works in later years led to recovery of many fossils from Olduvai Gorge and elsewhere in Tanzania and many are said to be in Germany. For example, a specimen code named OH 9 was at the Senckenberg Museum in Frankfurt am Main, Germany. A Tanzanian studied the material and in 1988, upon completion of his studies, he returned the specimen to Dar es Salaam, Tanzania.

4.2.2 Collected Animal Remains from Tanzania during German Rule

Recall, all scientific research endeavours were pioneered by Germans in Tanzania. A notable case is in Lindi region, south-eastern Tanzania. A mining Engineer, B. Sattler, who was in-charge of mining garnets under the company called Lindi Prospecting Company (Lindi Schürfgesellschaft) accidentally, noticed huge bone weathering exposed on land surface (Maier, 2003; Werner and Zils, 1997; Zils *et al.*, 1995). He informed his superiors in Germany and such measures later paved the way for intensive scientific investigations in the area (Maier, 2003; Werner and Zils, 1997; Zils *et al.*, 1995a, 1995b). Thus, at Tendaguru in Lindi region, south-eastern Tanzania, from 1907 to 1913 and from 1924 to 1931 profound discoveries of dinosaurs (now extinct) with one being the biggest ever (*Brachiosaurus brancai* later renamed as *Giraffatitan brancai*) that lived during those times (almost 160 million years ago) in Tanzania, along with other dinosaur as well as non-dinosaur remains were recovered (Maier, 2003; Magori and Saanane, 1998; Werner and Zils, 1997; Zils *et al.*, 1995a, 1995b).

Scientific expeditions in Tenduguru uncovered over 200 tonnes of fossils, majority of which were transported and stored at Museum für Naturkunde, Pläontologisches Institut, Berlin Germany, to date (Maier, 2003; Werner and Zils, 1997; Zils *et al.*, 1995, 1995b). Other reptilian remains, possibly belonging to turtle were recovered from Tendaguru (Maier, 2003).

Besides yielding dinosaur remains, evidence in the first Upper Jurassic mammalian remains is provided in Africa discovered from Tendaguru deposits (Maier, 2003; Zils, 1997; Zils *et al.*, 1995a, 1995b). The remains were examined and described by Wolf-Dieter Heinrich at the Museum of Natural History in Berlin (Maier, 2003; Magori and Saanane, 1998; Werner and Zils, 1997; Zils *et al.*, 1995, 1005b). Also, fish remains, assigned to *Lepidotus minor* were discovered from Tendaguru sediments (Maier, 2003; Magori and Saanane, 1998; Werner and Zils, 1997; Zils *et al.*, 1995). Invertebrates representing several species were recovered too at Tendaguru and thus, the sediments display marine horizons at that time (Maier, 2003; Werner and Zils, 1997; Zils *et al.*, 1995, 1995b).

4.2.3 Collected Plant Remains from Tanzania during German Rule

Moreover, plant (flora) remains in form of fossil pollen were recovered at Tendaguru horizons (Maier, 2003). They included marine dinoflagellate assemblage of the following groups: *Cicatricosisporites, Trisaccites* and *Ephedriites* (*ibid.*). The Tendaguru mission recovered also silicified wood in upper horizons of the deposits together with remains of immature cone likely from the family, *Araucariaceae*, species *Conites araucaroides* (*ibid.*). In sum, later recent studies on sediments stored in the museum facilitated for recovery of some 57 species of pollen that included 17 marine dinoflagellate palynomorphs, two fresh water algal forms, 12 pteridophyte and bryophyte representatives and 15 gymnosperm taxa (*ibid.*).

4.2.4 Collected Cultural Objects from Tanzania during German Rule

Recall, Chami and colleagues (2023) disclosed that some cultural materials were collected by Germans in Isanzu, Singida region. It was alleged by research participants that it was likely that some contemporary human remains, particularly skulls along with local equipment such as war fighting objects and ivory were the main items taken by Germans (*ibid.*). Such items are still in Germany (*ibid.*). Accordingly, it implies that besides human remains that were taken to Germany, ethnographic materials were taken to Germany such as those from Isanzu and they are still in Germany (*ibid.*)

4.3 Discussion: Repatriation Endeavours for Remains Collected from Tanzania during German Rule

4.3.1 Repatriated human remains from Germany (representing extant humans and extinct proto-humans)

Recall, almost 10,000 non-European human remains were kept in Berlin alone until after World War II (Stoecker and Winkelmann 2018; Winkelmann, 2020). Such number may have been close to 20,000 for Germany in total. By the time of Winkelmann's (2020) publication, 397 (2%) remains were repatriated to their places of origin around the world Winkelmann (2020). Notably, a number of human remains were acquired prior to formal beginning of German colonialism in 1884, nonetheless, the majority of repatriated remains were those obtained during the German Empire [(1871-1918) *ibid.*].

Chief Mkwawa's skull was returned to Tanzania during British colonial rule (Winkelmann, 2020; Le Gall, 2019; see Appendix I). According to Bucher (2016), on 19th July, 1954, by then Tanganyika (now mainland Tanzania) was under British rule, the Governor, Sir. Edward Twining attended the ceremony held at Kalenga in Iringa Township, Iringa region for returning the skull. The event celebrated Wahehe history and their chief, Mkwawa (Willoughby *et al.*, 2019). Additionally, the British Government established a memorial museum and mausoleum at Kalenga, where Mkwawa's skull including other materials plus few bullet casings shows Wahehe cultural history (*ibid.*). The museum at Kalenga under care of the Ministry of Natural Resources and Tourism is operational, to date.

After independence of Tanganyika, the government accorded the memorial museum of Kalenga national status in recognition to contribution of Chief Mkwawa (*ibid.*). Later on, in 1998, the first president of the United Republic of Tanzania, Julius Nyerere dedicated Freedom (*Uhuru* in Kiswahili) monument at Mlambalasi in commemoration of the centenary anniversary since death of Chief Mkwawa and officially acknowledged the role played by Mkwawa in resistance to German colonial rule (*ibid.*). The memorial was placed between the rock shelter, where Chief Mkwawa "… died and the cement tomb, which marks the burial location of his postcranial remains" (*ibid.*: 27).

In 1987, after completion of further analysis of Olduvai Hominid 9, belonging to proto-human *Homo ergaster* (*Homo erectus*), a Tanzanian, Dr. Abel Nkini returned the cranium to Tanzania (Maier and Nkini, 1984). Currently, the specimen is housed in Dar es Salaam at the National Museums of Tanzania. The specimen was discovered by Dr. Louis Leakey in 1960 (*ibid.*). It was recovered from sediments dated at about 1.4 million years ago (*ibid.*).

4.3.2 Un-repatriated human remains

The sub-section touches on another crux of the matter. As already illuminated in this chapter, quite a few materials that were taken to Germany have been repatriated. They include human remains representing living species; proto-human remains; non-human remains (plant and animal) and likely cultural objects as claimed by interviewed people of Isanzu, Singida region. With a big note is that all materials recovered from Tendaguru and shipped to Germany during colonial rule are yet to be repatriated to Tanzania.

4.3.3 Background to the stance on repatriation and Looming Questions

4.3.3.1 Background to the stance on repatriation

Recollect, all through the eighteenth to nineteenth centuries, there were particularly enormous displacements of cultural artifacts from colonized countries as consequences of punitive voyages, military plunders, or war tributes including those from trades as well as exchanges for collection intentions or to fulfil requirements of scientific research endeavours (Labadie, 2021).

Previously colonised countries and more lately local peoples obviously displayed enthusiasm to recover their heritage (*ibid.*). Nonetheless, scores of imperative remains are still spread out in museums of former colonial metropolitan areas and amongst private collectors (*ibid.*). Their demands are based on application of principles akin to those instituted in after effects of armed conflicts (*ibid.*). Besides, their requests are based on necessity to re-institute "… sacred links between people, territory and cultural heritage, and on a broader notion of the right to self-determination of peoples who must be able to revitalize and develop their cultural identity" (*ibid.*: 134).

Repatriation of cultural materials came out between countries during sixteenth and seventeenth centuries, though it is occasionally found in peace treaties signed in after conflicts, and in essence, it stems from political as well as diplomatic purposes (*ibid.*). At the onset of the nineteenth century, during the Congress of Vienna in 1815, the European countries too required France to return many archival materials and artworks seized by Napoleon's armies (*ibid.*). Many peace treaties wound up until the end of the nineteenth century had analogous repatriation clauses (*ibid.*). Signed peace at the terminal of the World War I nearly systematically had provisos relating to repatriation of plundered/pillaged artifacts or to reparation by materials of corresponding worth (*ibid.*).

After a lot of an ineffective compliance by various nations to the cause of repatriation of cultural materials to countries of origin, besides proviso protecting all properties of a civil nature, particular prohibition on looting cultural materials is recognized by The Hague Conventions of 1899 and 1907 (*ibid.*).

Besides, the conventions imposed a commitment on countries to guard against violation of that prevention (*ibid.*).

Moreover, the principle was preserved in the 1954 *Hague Convention for the Protection of Cultural Property in the Event of Armed Conflict* together with its two protocols that prevent export of artifacts from occupied territory and unequivocally oblige their return to the country from which they were taken (*ibid.*). Later on in 1970, the Convention on the Means of Prohibiting and Preventing the Illicit Import, Export and Transfer of Ownership of Cultural Property was adopted (*ibid.*). It obliges the international community to mobilize, at all times, against illicit trafficking of cultural materials (*ibid.*). Subsequently, in 1995, lack of a solution to take action to international disputes, the *UNIDROIT Convention on Stolen or Illegally Exported Cultural Objects* was adopted (*ibid.*). Developed at UNESCO's appeal, the convention aims to apply homogeneous treatment to demands for return of stolen or illegally exported cultural materials and pushes for United Nations member countries to standardize their legislations (*ibid.*).

Recently, some United Nations Security Council resolutions have plainly addressed the commitments of countries concerning repatriation of cultural materials illegally exported as a consequence of armed conflicts or terrorist activities (*ibid.*) Moreover, in 2006, the International Committee of the Red Cross ascertained that ban of plunder of cultural heritage and the commitment to return artifacts illegally exported from an occupied country fall under customary international law (*ibid.*). As a result, it applies to all countries, despite consequences of whether or not they ratified the aforesaid international instruments (*ibid.*).

Additionally, pertaining to local peoples, specifically the UN Declaration on the Rights of Indigenous Peoples, though not an obligatory instrument, it calls on countries to undertake reparation (*ibid.*). It may include compensation with regard to cultural materials that have been dispossessed (*ibid.*). Nonetheless, despite instituted international instruments concerning prevention of looting and commitment to return cultural materials, they often attest not enough to resolve demands relating to colonial period (*ibid.*).

The aforementioned international instruments are non-retroactive in nature (*ibid.*). Additionally, there are a variety of provisos that limit their capacity or extent (*ibid.*). For instance, The Hague Conventions of 1899 and 1907 are bound to circumstances of armed conflict between recognized countries, for the conventions exclude colonial conquests as well as wars of national liberation that did not qualify as interstate conflicts (*ibid.*).

Accordingly, European countries that benefited from colonialism more often than not used the International Law as a functional instrument for their expansionist interests (*ibid.*). Particularly, the concept "… of *terra nullius* served to justify their occupation, expropriation and looting of Indigenous peoples' lands around the world" (*ibid.*: 138).

The 1970 Convention is extremely narrow in extent, for instance, Article 7b, stipulates that "… the only cultural artifacts taken into consideration are those meeting the double criteria of coming from a museum (or similar *institution*), and of being inventoried" (*ibid.*: 137). As a result, the stipulation excludes cultural artifacts that have been/were "… subject of misappropriation before their registration, and those belonging to individuals or communities" (*ibid.*: 138).

At last, the UNIDROIT Convention allows requests for restitutions to benefit from a somewhat uniform judicial undertaking in a few UN member countries, but it has a time limit on requests for three years from the moment the plaintiff has all pieces of information necessary to proceed with a legal action and, in all scenarios, of 50 years from the date of theft (*ibid.*). There are few exceptions provided by The Convention to such limit concerning "… cultural artifacts forming an integral part of an identified monument or archaeological site, artifacts belonging to a public collection, and cultural artifacts used by a tribal or Indigenous community as part of that community's traditional or ritual use" (*ibid*: 138).

4.3.4 Looming Questions

Owing to stance on scanty materials that have been repatriated to Tanzania, the following questions are at the centre-stage:

Owing to unclear aspects about what was taken and what was not taken, as informed, for instance, by respondents in Chami and colleagues' study in Isanzu, Singida region, Tanzania what materials were shipped to German during colonial rule? That goes together on whereabouts of many likely unknown human, cultural objects including other material remains stored in Germany like Mangi Meli of Kilimanjaro and others from elsewhere in Tanzania such that what is the way forward to their repatriation? What is their fate? Who are in possession of such materials? Are they academic institutions, public as well private (universities, museums), or private individuals? Are there scientific collaborations between German and Tanzanian scientists and technicians?

However, there are some positive moves towards repatriation of materials taken from Tanzania. Several initiatives from Tanzania, for example, by the retired president, Honourable Jakaya Mrisho Kikwete made calls for repatriation of Tendaguru remains, particularly dinosaur remains. In 2019, a memorandum of understanding (MoU) to that effect was signed between Natural History Museum Berlin and the University of Dar es Salaam together with the National Museums of Tanzania. The question that arises is that, what is the status of such tri-partite collaboration?

Moreover, the President of the Federal Republic of Germany visited Tanzania at the end of 2023. He even travelled to Songea and visited the Songea Majimaji War Memorial Museum. Besides, officials in the region, he met local people including family members (grandchildren) of Chief Songea Mbano and apologised on behalf of the German people for atrocities they did to people during Majimaji war. He promised for a positive direction towards repatriation of remains including reparation. The question is how far are measures on both German and Tanzanian sides?

4.4 Future Prospects

Even though there is no international legal commitment to return cultural materials acquired during the colonial period, their repatriation is a moral duty and comes from logic of commitment to repair long-ago injustices (see Labadie, 2021). Chami and colleagues (2023) offer a piece of advice that in dealing with such problem, there should be wisdom, negotiation and agreement. Such measures should include establishment or identification of an institution to supervise the demands (*ibid.*).

Other moves could be voluntary donations or restitutions, while other measures could be mediation or arbitration (Labadie, 2021). Nonetheless, the latter moves are prone to problems that must be carefully executed. For instance, judges as well as lawyers must be ready to face complex practical including procedural undertakings with the aim of identifying the applicable law, nonetheless, there could be repeatedly unpredictable results (*ibid.*).

All in all, the two countries have firm/strong diplomatic ties with cooperation between government bodies and private entities/individuals for socio-economic developments. There are major funding facilitations to development projects in Tanzania. Besides, there have been and there is still, academic cooperation with Tanzanians gaining study scholarships at diverse avenues. For example, they are bestowed scholarship for post-graduate studies, post-doctorate studies and research. Also, there are academic exchange measures between universities of the two countries both public and private.

There is government will on both sides, Federal Government of Germany and United Republic of Tanzania, on aspirations to repatriate and undertake reparation for materials collected by Germans during their colonial rule. Accordingly, this is the window of hope for such positive motives. After all, Germany has been and still, offers sponsorship for training Tanzanians such that there is room for carrying out reparation of materials by using wisdom, negotiations and agreements at both government level, and where need be, particularly for human remains, undertake such measures mutually to grass root level, the community or communities involved.

References

Bucher, J. (2016). "The skull of Mkwawa and the politics of indirect rule in Tanganyika." *Journal of East African Studies*, 10(2): 284-302.

Chami, Maximilian, F., Simba, Alma and Stoecker, Holger (2023). "Community Awareness and Restitution of Isanzu Ancestors' Human Remains from the University of Göttingen Collections to Mkalama District, Tanzania." Africa Spectrum, 58(2): 155–178.

Crema, E.(2004). *Wahehe a Bantu People*. Grafiche Sedram, San Vito al Tagliamento.

Iliffe, Rob (2003). "Science and Voyages of Discovery." In *The Cambridge History of Science*. Roy Porter ed. Cambridge: Cambridge University Press. Pp 618-646.

Iliffe, J. (1979). *A modern history of Tanganyika*. Cambridge: University Press, Cambridge.

Kayombo, N. A. (2005). "Management of movable heritage in Tanzania." In B. B. Mapunda and P. Msemwa P (eds). *Salvaging Tanzania's Cultural Heritage*. Dar es Salaam: Dar es Salaam Press, pp. 271–278.

Labadie, Camille (2021)."Decolonizing collections: A legal perspective on the restitution of cultural artifacts," *ICOFOM Study Series* [Online], 49-2 | 2021, DOI: https://doi.org/10.4000/iss.3784.

Lawrence, Christopher. (2015). "18th and 19th Century European Expeditions." Megan Ward and Adrian S. Wisnicki, eds. *Livingstone*

Online. http://livingstoneonline.org/uuid/node/c97b074f-908e-4022-8ce9-e23418a99796

Magori, Cassian and Saanane, Charles (1998). *Dinosaria wa Tendauru*. Dar es Salaam: E & D Limited.

Maier, Gerhard (2003). *African Dinosaurs Unearthed: The Tendaguru Expeditions*, Bloomington IN: Indiana University Press.

Maier, W. and Nkini, A. (1984). "Olduvai Hominid 9: New Results of Investigation." Courier Forschungsinstiut Senckenberg. 69: 123-130.

Matu, M., Crevecoeur, I. and Huchet, J.-B. (2017). "Taphonomy and Paleoichnology of Olduvai Hominid 1 (OH1), Tanzania." *International Journal of Osteoarchaeology*. DOI: 10.1002/oa.2593.

Maughan, Steven (n.d.). "Explorers, Missionaries, Traders." Encyclopaedia of European Social History. Retrieved 2024 www. Enclopaedia.com/international

Monson, J. (2000). "Memory, Migration and the Authority of History in Southern Tanzania, 1860-1960." *The Journal of African History*, 41(3): 347-372.

Musso, M. (2011). *Mukwavinyika Mwamuyinga na kabila lake la Hehe*. 2nd edition, Dar es Salaam: Dar es Salaam University Press.

Perras A (2004). *Carl Peters and German Imperialism 1856-1918: A Political Biography*. Oxford: Clarendon Press. ISBN 9780199265107. OCLC 252667062.

Redmayne, A. (1968). "Mkwawa and the Hehe Wars." *Journal of African History*, 9(3): 409-436.

Redmayne, A. (1970). "The War Trumpets and Other Mistakes in the History of the Hehe." *Anthropos*, 65: 98-109.

Le Gall, Yann (2019). "Remembering the Dismembered African Human Remains and Memory Cultures in and after Repatriation." A thesis submitted in fulfilment of the requirements for the degree of Doctor of Philosophy as part of the Research Training Group "Minor Cosmopolitanisms" at the University of Potsdam.

Rushohora, Nancy Alexander (2019). "Graves, Houses of Pain and Execution: Memories of the German Prisons after the Majimaji War in Tanzania (1904–1908)." *The Journal of Imperial and Commonwealth History*, 47(2): 275-299, DOI: 10.1080/03086534.2019.1605697

Rushohora, Nancy Alexander (2015). "An Archaeological Identity of the Majimaji: Towards an Historical Archaeology of Resistance to German Colonisation in Southern Tanzania." PhD Thesis, University of Pretoria.

Stoecker, H. and Winkelmann, A. (2018) "Skulls and skeletons from Namibia in Berlin – Results of the Charité Human Remains Project." *Human Remains and Violence*, 4 (2): 5-26.

Werner, C. and Zils, W. (1997). "The Tendaguru Expedition December 1996." Terra Nostra 7(97): 28-32.

Willoughby, Pamela R., Biittner Katie M., Bushozi Pastory M., and Miller Jennifer M. Miller (2019). "A German Rifle Casing and Chief Mkwawa of the Wahehe: the Colonial and Post-Colonial Significance of Mlambalasi Rockshelter, Iringa Region, Tanzania." Journal *of African Archaeology*, 17: 23-35. DOI: 10.1163/21915784-20190004

Winkelmann, Andreas (2020). "Repatriations of human remains from Germany – 1911 to 2019." *Museum & Society*, 18(1) 40-51.

Zils, W., Werner, C., Moritz, A. & Saanane, C. (1995a). "Tendaguru the Most Famous Locality of Africa. Review Survey and Future Prospects." DOCUMENTA NATURAE 97:1-41; MUNICH.

Zils, W., Werner, C., Moritz, A. and Saanane, C. (1995b). Orientierende Tendauguru Expedition 1994." Berliner Geowissenschaftliche Abhandlungen 16(2): 483-531.

APPENDICES

Overview of repatriations of colonially acquired human remains from Germany (including Mkwawa's Skull)

Year	Institution	Number of individuals	Community	Nation	References
1911	Royal Ethnological Museum Berlin	2	?	Samoa	Zimmerman 2001: 161
1954	Übersee-Museum Bremen	1	Hehe	Tanzania	Baer and Schröter 2001*
1978	Göttingen University	2	Shuar	Ecuador	Magisches Einsatzkommando der Deutschen Gesellschaft für Völkerkunde 1978
1991	Ethnological Museum Hamburg	1	Maori	New Zealand	Te Papa Museum 2011: 5
2006	Übersee-Museum Bremen	2	Maori	New Zealand	Fründt and Förster 2018; Herewini 2008
2011	Charité Berlin	20	Herero, Nama	Namibia	Stoecker and Winkelmann 2018*; Winkelmann 2012
2011	Institute of Anatomy Bonn	1	Krenak	Brasil	
2011	Senckenberg Museum Frankfurt	1	Maori	New Zealand	Te Papa Museum 2011: 4
2011	Weltkulturen Museum Frankfurt	1	Maori	New Zealand	Te Papa Museum 2011: 5

2012	Charité Berlin	1	Aché	Paraguay	Koel-Abt and Winkelmann 2013*
2012	State Ethnological Museum Munich	1	?	Peru	
2013	Charité Berlin	33	Aborigine	Australia	Winkelmann 2020*; Winkelmann and Teßmann 2013*
2014	Charité Berlin	21	Damara, Herero, Nama, Ovambo, San	Namibia	Stoecker and Teßmann 2013*; Stoecker and Winkelmann 2018*; Winkelmann and Stoecker 2014
2014	Charité Berlin	14	Aborigine, Torres Strait Islander	Australia	Winkelmann 2020*
2014	Charité Berlin	1	Tasmanian Aborigine	Australia	Winkelmann and Teßmann 2018*
2014	Freiburg University	14	Herero, Nama, Damara	Namibia	Möller 2015[2008]; Wittwer-Backofen et al. 2014*
2014	Private	1**	Hehe	Tanzania	Brockmeyer 2018
2017	Charité Berlin	1	Aborigine	Australia	Winkelmann 2020*
2017	BGAEU	1	Ngadjon	Australia	
2017	Senckenberg Gesellschaft für Naturforschung Frankfurt	1	Aborigine	Australia	Schrenk et al. 2018: 51
2017	Übersee-Museum Bremen	44	Maori, Moriori	New Zealand	

2017	BGAEU	1	Ainu	Japan	
2017	State Ethnographic Collections Saxony	4	Hawai'i	USA	Ayau and Keeler 2017
2017	Landesmuseum Hannover	1	Lamalama	Australia	
2018	Charité Berlin	17**	Herero, Nama, Ovambo, San	Namibia	Stoecker and Winkelmann 2018*
	Private	1	?	Namibia	Ziegenfuß and Rücker 2018*
	Institute of Anatomy Greifswald	3	Herero, Nama	Namibia	
	Jena University	1	Herero?	Namibia	Förster and Stoecker 2016*
	University Medical Center Hamburg	1	?	Namibia	
	DITSL Witzenhausen	1	Nama	Namibia	Hulverscheidt and Stoecker 2018*; Hulverscheidt et al. 2017*
	Landesmuseum Hannover	3	Nama	Namibia	
2018	Rautenstrauch-Joest-Museum Cologne	1	Maori	New Zealand	
2019	Fünf Kontinente-Museum Munich	1	Yidindji	Australia	Turnbull 2017: 2, 263

2019	Linden-Museum Stuttgart	2	Aborigine	Australia	
	Freiburg University	8	Aborigine	Australia	
2019	State Ethnographic Collections Saxony	76	Aborigine, incl. Yawuru	Australia	Schlott 2018; Skyring and Yu 2019*
	Institute of Anatomy Halle	5	Aborigine, incl. Biyaygirri	Australia	
2019	Charité Berlin	109	Maori, Moriori	New Zealand	

Source: Winkelmann (2020).

Key: BGAEU = Berliner Gesellschaft für Anthropologie, Ethnologie und Urgeschichte (Berlin Society for Anthr

CHAPTER FIVE

GERMAN BUILT HERITAGE FOR CONTINUED USE FOR SOCIO-ECONOMIC DEVELOPMENT IN TANZANIA

By Charles Bernard Saanane

5.0 Introduction

This chapter presents important aspects on German built heritage for continued use for socio-economic development in Tanzania. It is important due to several reasons. Built heritage resources developed during German rule are still in use because they have been and they are still being restored, maintained and conserved. Importantly, such measures, to a great extent, keep their historic fabric, value, authenticity and thus, their continued use permit activation of their potential as dynamic resources that serve the government (for inherited assets) and local people's needs including government use. The built heritage resources include tangible cultural as well as intangible heritage assets that are in use in offering social services such as education, health care, worship and Kiswahili language, while others are for trade via transportation networks like railway system, roads, ports/harbours and customs ware houses.

Before setting on description of sections, there is a brief overview showing that Tanganyika (now mainland Tanzania) was under German colonial rule. This is followed by rationale for the presentation. This chapter has the following sections: Infrastructure for Socio-Economic Services; Economic Ventures; Establishment and Development of Transport Infrastructure; Establishment of Trade Centres; Establishment of Social Services; Kiswahili Language; Research and Development; Discussion; and Future Prospects.

General Overview

After the Berlin conference in 1884, owing to division of Africa into domains of power, German ruled Togo, Cameroon, Namibia (then German South-West Africa) and German East Africa that comprised the current Burundi, Rwanda and Tanganyika, currently known as mainland Tanzania (Larson, 2021). In pursuit of its administration, Germany established settlements for administrative and socio-economic development. Accordingly, they established infrastructure in form of road network; railway; houses for administration, residence, schools, health care as well as worship (by Christian missionaries); and plantations. Many Germany establishments were and still are being used in independent Tanganyika (currently, mainland Tanzania) for socio-economic development.

Rationale for the Presentation

The presentation is anchored on utilisation of a pertinent cognitive frame of reference, which is specifically free from bias. It offers a safe haven for offering open standing perspectives on the subject matter, which appears, to a certain extent, neglected in scholarship. It is the untold truth. Accordingly, such cognitive frame of reference, which is important, is none other than Afrocentricity Theory. Genesis and development of Afrocentricity Theory owe greatly to outcomes from Pan-Africanism and Nationalism (Watson, 2015; Shockley & Frederick, 2010). The first person to employ the framework as the suitable paradigm was the first president of independent Ghana, the late Kwame Nkrumah in the 1960s and it was later given the biggest impetus by Professor Molefi Kete Asante (Watson, 2015).

Briefly, as a cognitive frame of reference, Afrocentricity Theory connotes for re-centering African organization from objects to participants in history (Khokholkova, 2016). According to Asante's initial definition, the framework means African-centered as positioning of African morals or ethics (ideals) at the center of any analysis that engrosses African culture and behaviour (Bangura, 2012). Of special note is that the theory should not be confused with the term Afrocentrism (*ibid.*). The latter is beyond the scope of discussion in this chapter.

Outstandingly, following Asante's supposition, Afrocentricity Theory, in its application, neither opposes any racial grouping nor supports any kind of discrimination (Watson, 2015). Accordingly, Afrocentricity Theory insists on diversity of cultural stances as well as comprehensions with no social stratum and specifically without referring to a person being better than another or highly advanced compared to the other (*ibid.*).

In due regard, anchored on its outstanding premises, Afrocentricity Theory is pertinent for applying in the presented materials in this chapter. It is safe to argue that German built heritage in Tanzania is undeniably important to the country's current use for socio-economic development. It is centred on the fact that the said built heritage does not denigrate Tanzania's stance on its continued use and maintenance. It encompasses tangible heritage (infrastructure of many forms) and intangible heritage, notably the up-graded Kiswahili used from olden times including during German rule, to date, for official government use, national language and medium of instruction at elementary education level (primary school).

5.1 Infrastructure for Socio-Economic Services

5.1.1 Houses for Governance and Settlements

In the 1880s, Bagamoyo town located along the coast almost 70 kilometres north of Dar es Salaam city had settlements and it was the main port that handled a lot of import including export of trade items (Kironde, 1994). Then German East African Company stayed in Bagamoyo before the German government installed its rule in the country (*ibid.*). Accordingly, in location for initial governance, German government rulers who took over from the German East African Company had to construct buildings for their institutions of governance.

Bagamoyo that was initially the capital of German ruke in Tanganyika had some government buildings that included an old fort, which was a German administration building (known in Kiswahili as *boma*), German storehouse and second old German boma (Mosha and Plevoets, 2020). During the outbreak of an uprising against German rule by Arabs under direction of Abushiri, the old fort was used by Germans as an army barrack for several years (Mosha and Plevoets, 2020; Brenan and Burton, 2007). Later, it was used as a leaders' residence but it was converted to state house (Lucian, 2019). The authority used Bagamoyo as its capital for few years and in 1891, owing to its shallow Ocean depth, they moved as well as relocated their seat of governance - where the ocean shore is deaper than Bagamoyo - south to Mzizima [(presently known as Dar es Salaam) Lucian, 2019; Kironde, 1994].

The Old Boma building, including other historic buildings in Bagamoyo, is owned as well as operated by the government of Tanzania (Lucian, 2019).

As the government seat was moved to Dar es Salaam that also became the chief port, the town embraced territorial and district government authorities (Mosha and Plevoets, 2020; Kirey, 2020; Kironde, 1994). In the 1890s, construction of the Governor's palace together with numerous government buildings was on-going in Dar es Salaam (Kironde, 1994). The newly established government seat in Dar es Salaam had the District Office *(Bezirksamt)* that was built close to the *Boma,* along with a prison *(gefingnis)* and a local court [*(schaurihutte) ibid.*]. Additionally, the government planned as well as developed land into office buildings, commercial structures, warehouses, roads, open spaces, transportation alley ways and so forth *(ibid.).* Besides, in planned land areas, the government designated land parcels into administrative area, residential areas, port area together with customs and, to a certain degree, commercial area *(ibid.).* Accordingly, the current set-up of Dar es Salaam (now a city and the main Tanzanian commercial hub) is adjustment and development of land areas including continued use of old buildings constructed by Germans like Old Boma, which is named as City Hall is used by the Dar es Salaam City authority for its offices. In Dar es Salaam, the building that was used by the German governor was renovated as well as conserved and it is still used by the government as the state house.

Additionally, owing to establishment of port infrastructure in Dar es Salaam and central railway construction that was connected to the port, railway construction involved erection of buildings starting from Dar es Salaam to Kigoma port along Lake Tanganyika shores (Mosha and Plevoets, 2020). Thus, there are houses, mainly stations as well as staff houses, along the railway infrastructure from Dar es Salaam and thus, in Morogoro, Dodoma, Tabora to Kigoma. All are operational, to date.

The German authority gradually established its administration in the country such that in 1891, it set up four administrative districts along the coast and by 1903, the country was subdivided into 12 as well as 16 military districts (Kironde, 1994). Nonetheless, in 1914, owing to calm after many resistances that led to wars, military districts were increased to 24 accompanied by reduction of military districts to two at Mahenge and Iringa (Larson, 2021; Kironde, 1994). Dar es Salaam was amongst the early districts to be set-up (Kironde, 1994).

In devolution of the central government roles, there was introduction of local administration under the rubric Communial Unions (*Kommunal*

Verbandes) in several districts (*ibid.*). They included Tanga, Pangani, Bagamoyo, Kilwa, Lindi, Wilhelmstall (currently called Lushoto), Kilosa, Mbeya Langemburg (currently called Mbeya) and Dar es Salaam (*ibid.*). They were mandated with duties that encompassed to set up schools, street lighting, waste collection, drainage of swamps, road as well as bridge construction, allotment of seeds to local people and supervision of cooperative village farms (*ibid.*). Several unions were set-up in the country and in Dar es Salaam, there was established Dar es Salaam Union that had a special task of guarantee to the early Savings Bank (*ibid.*). Nevertheless, many unions were brought to an end and kept unions of Tanga and Dar es Salaam with highly partial authority and they were confined to residential areas (*ibid.*). In 1908 and 1909, there was a notion of set up of Municipal Councils (*Stadtgemaindes*) that were to be mandated for maintenance of roads as well as public spaces; water supply; street lighting; cleaning; refuse disposal; and school upkeep (*ibid.*). But by the end of their rule in 1918, only Dar es Salaam and Tanga had Municipal Council status (*ibid.*).

Owing to historical and architectural significance together with continued use of buildings constructed by Germans in Dar es Salaam city, the Antiquities Division declared part of such heritage as an Architectural Conserved Area (Kigadye, 2014). The area is 0.4642 kilometre squares (*ibid.*). It embraces the area between Ocean Road, Chimara Road, Shaaban Robert Street, Sokoine Drive, Azikiwe Street and Kivukoni Front (*ibid.*).

Developments were also in other towns like Arusha where constructed houses were for government use. There is the Old Boma that was a military station. Currently, the complex houses the public institution, Arusha National Natural History Museum as the branch of the National Museums of Tanzania. Besides, in many towns where there was German administration, houses were constructed. For example, in Mtwara Mikindani, there is the Old Boma currently in use as a hotel and there are several buildings in the vicinity.

5.1.2 Electricity Services

According to Kironde (1994), after 1905, there was minimal electricity supply in Dar es Salaam town. The works for such utility supply was carried out by East Africa Railroad Company (Edward and Hård, 2020; Kironde (1994). Supply was directed at railways, several hotels and streets where Europeans dwelled (Kironde, 1994).

5.2 Economic Ventures

5.2.1 Establishment of Ports, Warehouses and Customs Services

There were established ports at Dar es Salaam (the chief port), Tanga in Tanga region; Pangani as well as Bagamoyo in Pwani region; Kilwa Kivinje together with Lindi in Lindi region; and Mikindani in Mtwara region (Kironde, 1994). Further harbour developments at Dar es Salaam port were carried out in 1905 by constructing a quay at the northern part (*ibid.*). Such improvement was intended to assist and enlarge facilities for freight discharge as well as loading (*ibid.*).

A floating dock was not completed at Dar es Salaam harbour till 1901, but by August, 1901, it sunk by accident. It was floated to surface and started work in January 1902. By 1904, it was realised that in fact the dock was very small and could not handle any, but two of the smallest ships of the German East African Line, which had domination over the Dar es Salaam port.

Customs and Warehousing

Several warehouses as well as customs structures were initially set up at Dar es Salaam port (Kironde, 1994). Besides, there were facelifts at the Dar es Salaam port that went along during railway construction and included a highly equipped dockyard south of the port (*ibid.*). Also, between 1892 and 1894, there was construction of a lighthouse at Dar es Salaam port (*ibid.*).

Importantly, in 891, the German authority set up the Customs Department along ports that operated as presented in the previous sub-section (*ibid.*). The headquarters were in Dar es Salaam (*ibid.*). For control of imports and exports, there was construction of customs structures (*Zo/Iamt, Zollamtagen*) along Dar es Salaam port (*ibid.*).

5.2.2 Establishment of Plantations

The government arranged the country by setting up separate export-producing areas (Enns and Bersaglio, 2020). Coffee plantations were set up in mountainous areas in Kilimanjaro region, north-eastern Tanzania (*ibid.*). Sisal and rubber production were extended as well as set up in central Tanzania, while new types of cotton and tobacco were established in western Tanzania for small holders (*ibid.*).

African peasants surpassed German settler farmers in cotton production by 1906 (Kironde, 1994). In 1908, cotton export as a result of African peasant production was over two-thirds (*ibid.*). In 1912, it was recorded to account for five sevenths of its production for export (*ibid.*).

After some years, local people became self-sufficient in terms of agriculture (Larson, 2021). For instance, people in Tabora as well as Mahenge in Morogoro were beneficiaries of self-sufficient agricultural undertakings (*ibid.*). They augmented banana cultivation as a cash crop (*ibid.*).

5.2.3 Mining

Mineral exploration by Germans revealed occurrence of the following minerals in Tanzania: mica, copper, iron, lead, iron and zinc (Bryceson *et al.*, 2012). In 1898, Koncession fur Edelmineralien, a Germany company discovered gold at Sangura Hill located 15 kilometres from Geita town, Geita region, north-western Tanzania (*ibid.*). Additionally, during German rule in 1906, gold was discovered at Senkenke in Singida region and extraction started in 1909 (Bryceson *et al.*, 2012; Magai and Márquez-Velázquez, 2011). In 1907, the mining entity extracted one ton of gold with a big workforce (Bryceson *et al.*, 2012). Currently, mining works in independent Tanzania are carried out by broadening scope and variety of minerals established by previous rulers [(Germans and later the British) Bryceson *et al.*, 2012; Magai and Márquez-Velázquez, 2011].

5.2.4 Wildlife Conservation Measures

Wildlife conservation was practised by local people before arrival of foreigners in Tanzania and thus, they were and still they are wildlife conservators. They were involved in hunting for their own use but owing to their small population size, they never reduced the wild game counts (Baldus, 2001). As pioneer wildlife conservators, they had their own established cultural practices for control of depletion of wild game species counts including environmental conservation measures (*ibid.*). They used taboos that prohibited hunting of particular animal species and hunting was permissible during defined seasons of the year (*ibid.*). Moreover, such conservation measures embraced several forest conservation by regarding them, which prohibited tree cutting and animal hunting (*ibid.*).

In later centuries, arrival of Arabs with their slave trade and hunting for ivory were carried out together in the country (*ibid.*). Such illicit trade patterns denigrated local people's wildlife and environmental conservation measures instituted through time immemorial.

Furthermore, before German rule in the country, there was commercial hunting by many people from a variety of nations and mainly, they were from South Africa (Baldus, 2001). They hunted for sale locally and abroad for a variety of needs and included animal by-products such as ivory, skins, horns and meat (*ibid.*). Meat was sold to local people in close proximity to hunting areas (*ibid.*).

During German rule, commercial hunting continued. Notably, out of such practices, from 1903 to 1911, 256 tons of ivory were exported and sold overseas (Baldus, 2001). Moreover, during the same period, 53 tons of rhinocerous horns were exported for sale abroad (*ibid.*). Besides, thousands of live anmilas encompassed export of 50 tons of antelope horns and 2.7 tons of bird feathers (*ibid.*).

Owing to such wildlife malpractices, in 1896, the German Governor issued the first general Wildlife Ordinance (*ibid.*). Additionally, decrees were issued by the German authority in 1898, 1900, 1903, 1905 and 1908 that eventually led to formulation as well as issuance of the Hunting Act in 1911 (*ibid.*). That was the first legislation in the country pertaining to control of illicit practices to wild game. The Act shows that it protected several animals and it was enacted due to threat to animals in the country after many immigrants who were hunters by then, for instance, Selous, Schillings and Schomburgk (*ibid.*). They opposed such legislation but it was meant for stoppage of all commercial culling and regulated hunting (*ibid.*).

The Hunting Act of 1911 forbade killing of birds, for instance, ostriches, vultures, secretary birds and owls (*ibid.*). Also, the Act forbade collection of eggs from the enlisted birds (*ibid.*). Besides, it provided full protection of chimpanzees and all female including young wild animals (*ibid.*). Of course other animal species were relegated to categories of various full protective measures and they were required to be hunted based on curbed hunting licenses (*ibid.*). Moreover, the government had powers to close some areas if they were envisaged to experience hunting thrust from lust hunters (*ibid.*).

Granting of hunting license was free to local people as well as foreigners. However, hunting of elephants had special restrictions of hunting only two elephants in a year for those with such license (*ibid.*). Such paid for hunting licenses were non-refundable (*ibid.*). Besides, former convicts of hunting offences were not awarded hunting licenses and such licenses could be re-claimed by the government (*ibid.*). On one hand, landholders were permitted to shoot animals for protection of their lives as well as properties but if it happened, they were required to surrender skins and tusks to the government (*ibid.*). On the other hand, predator species such as lions, leopards, wild dogs and crocodiles were hunted freely and they were hunted for a reward (*ibid.*).

In its pursuit to wildlife conservation, by 1911, the German government declared 15 protected areas that were almost 30,000 kilometre squares or 5 percent of Tanzania [Baldus, 2001; United Republic of Tanzania (URT), 2007]. They were the first wildlife protected areas in the country. By 1896, before legislation of 1911, they included set up of Rufiji currently known as Selous and on west side of Kilimanjaro Mountain (Baldus, 2001). All protected areas by then were known as Hunting Reserves but hunting was forbidden in such areas (*ibid.*). Fines were imposed on a person who hunted illegally and they depended on animal species illegally hunted (*ibid.*). Accordingly, four game reserves were located along Rufiji River (in Pwani region) and Ruaha River (in Iringa region) as well as close to Liwale and Lindi, all in Lindi region (*ibid.*).

5.3 Establishment and Development of Transport Infrastructure

Priority for infrastructure development in th country was deemed to enhance extraction, production including passage of materials efficiently (Enns and Bersaglio, 2020). Accordingly, it supported capital passage and thus, permitted rulers' full economic prospective of people and the country (*ibid.*). Also, the Germans installed a ship, M.V. Liemba that plied and it still plies in Lake Tanganyika waters between points including neigbouring Democratic Republic of Congo. The vessel has been in use up to independent Tanzania. It has been getting maintance fo its continued use.

5.3.1 Railways Construction, Post and Telegraph Stations

According to Edward and Hård (2020), railways, roads, post as well as telegraph stations were built. The Central Line was started to be constructed in 1905 and it was completed in 1914 (Enns and Bersaglio, 2020; Mosha and Plevoets, 2020). The railway was built from Dar es Salaam to Kigoma and it followed the Central Caravan route used by early traders before German took over to rule the country (Enns and Bersaglio, 2020). Railway construction was broadened in 1912 from Dar es Salaam to Tanga and Moshi line (Greiner, 2022; Kangalawe, 2021). The railway network is still in use, to date.

5.3.2 Road construction

Up to 1901, roads to and from the interior were still very poor. Construction of roads was initiated by German rulers and they transformed footpaths into roads and they started such road works by 1893 (Greiner, 2022). In the terminal 1880s and early 1900s, the authority set up a road network that started from Dar es Salaam port (Brenan and Burton, 2007). Road works were mainly targeted for Tanga and Dar es Salaam towns by 1893 but in 1896, they stopped due to lack of funds (Greiner, 2022). However, after acquiring funds, road works started in 1897 from Kilwa and Lindi to the hinterland, while resumption of such works was started at the same time for roads out of Dar es Salaam (*ibid.*). Also, new roads were planned between Lake Nyasa in the south and Lake Tanganyika in the west plus between Tabora and Mwanza along Lake Victoria (*ibid.*).

5.4 Establishment of Social Services

5.4.1 Establishment of Schools

Bagamoyo was the first place to build a school during German rule. A government owned, Mwambao Primary School in Bagamoyo was estblished in 1892 (Mosha and Plevoets, 2020). According to Brenan and Burton (2007), in 1895, in Dar es Salaam, the first government school was established.

Furthermore, owing to failure to attract many Africans in Dar es Salaam metropolitan centre, Catholic and Non-Catholic Christian missions established schools in outskirts of Dar es Salaam. On one hand, in 1893, well before the Benedictine missionaries, Evangelical missionaries established their school at Kisarawe in Pwani region (Brenan and Burton, 2007). On the other hand, in 1896, Benedictine missionaries (Catholic) set up at Kurasini a mixed boarding school for girls and boys whereby enrollment at the school reached 73 girls and 100 boys (*ibid.*).

As it will be presented later, all schools used Kiswahili as the medium of instruction. They trained local people in literary subjects and vocational as well as technical education. Local people were trained so as to be employed by the government for casual labour and similarly, they were employed in private plantation farms.

5.4.2 Establishment of Healthcare Facilities

As already presented on aspects concerning house construction by German rulers, particularly in Bagamoyo, old Sewa Haji hospital was set up in 1912 (Mosha and Plevoets, 2020). According to Bendix (2012), in 1897, the German authority established Ocean Road Hospital in Dar es Salaam. The hospital, is still in use and currently, the country's sole Cancer Institute, was given a facelift in the end of 1990s as a result of cooperation with the German Cancer Research Center in Heidelberg together with sponsorship through a private scheme, Tanzania Tumor Aid Association Heidelberg e.V. (*ibid.*).

Besides the German goverment authority's establishment of healthcare facilities in the country, Christian missionaries established several health facilities across the country. In 1909, Benedictine missionaries at Kwiro in Mahenge, Morogoro region requested for set up of a joint government and mission leprosy project (Larson, 2021). The place was named Tabora Christian Missionary and it started being operational before the First World War with involvement of local district authority (*ibid.*). Also, in 1913, at Mwena close to Ndanda in Masasi, Mtwara region, missionaries started handling leprosy patients (*ibid.*). Furthermore, there were two additional centres for leprosy treatments operated by Benedictine missionaries at Madibira and Peramiho in Ruvuma region (*ibid.*). Besides, after the situation became very difficult to handle patients, another centre (the fourth under Benedctines) was established later (*ibid.*). Other centres under Benedictines were established that included Lukuledi in 1895 as well as Nyangao, all in Lindi region; Tosamanganga (1897) in Iringa region; and Madibira (1897), Peramiho (1898) as well as Kigonsera (1898) in Ruvuma region (*ibid.*).

5.5 Kiswahili Language

Kiswahili language was a result of initial interactions between local people along the coast and foreigners, the Arabs. It was mostly blended with words from Bantu languages and Arabic. According to Malik (1996), it was influential in teachings of Islam, which was later spread to inland of Tanzania (*ibid.*). Also, it was instrumental as well as a significant language of trade in local long distance trade routes for slavery, ivory and other trade commodities from the coast to the hinterland areas, for instance, seashore towns of Pangani, Bagamoyo, Kilwa and later Dar es Salaam to inland trade centres, such as Njombe, Tabora and Ujiji (*ibid.*).

In the nineteenth century when Explorers arrived to Tanzania, they encountered local people, especially those along coastal areas and local long distance trade centres using Kiswahili as the *lingua franca* (*ibid.*). Similarly, early Christian missionaries had to learn and converse in already established Kiswahili language along the entry points, coastal towns and alongside long distance trade centres (*ibid.*). Accordingly, for spread of Christianity, they used Kiswahili language (*ibid.*).

Later on in the nineteenth century, Kiswahili was a helpful tool for use for strengthening German rule and as already presented, it was useful for spread of Christianity in inland areas (*ibid.*). It was not a normal form of communication by many people, but European missionaries together with set up of German administration facilitated to use Kiswahili as the medium of communication (*ibid.*). During German rule in the country, Kiswahili language became a powerful instrument for cultural, economic and political transformation (*ibid.*). Such stance owed to the fact that early Catholic and Protestant missionaries who arrived to Tanzania before German rule set up schools, particularly in coastal areas and used Kiswahili among study subjects together with technical instructions (*ibid.*).

Accordingly, in 1890s, German rule chose use of Kiswahili as an official language in support of their administration around the country (*ibid.*). In so doing, the German authority enhanced standing of Kiswahili and offered Kiswahili knowledge new significance away from coastal areas including trade centres of Tanzania (*ibid.*). Later, the German authority extended funding to missionary schools because of their technical skills training and language so that they could employ skills as well as skilled persons in the fast growing administration (*ibid.*).

It is important to note that spread of Kiswahili in the country owed much to impetus accorded by the German administration at diverse capacities (*ibid.*). Books were made available, for example, they encompassed a grammar book by Krapf published in 1850, his Kiswahili dictionary, which was published in 1882 and a Handbook by Edward Steere published in 1870 (*ibid.*). Another added dimension for spread of Kiswahili in government schools was evident in legendary subjects, vocational education including technical education and it dispatched away from Islamic oral as well as literary tradition that enhanced people's acceptance of its usage as medium of communication (*ibid.*).

Besides, further spread of Kiswahili language was facilitated by appointment of Kiswahili-speaking officers at their grassroots governance levels in the country (*ibid.*). They were known as Akida and Jumbe in Kiswahili and they were posted across the country (*ibid.*). They employed people who could speak Kiswahili as manual workers for government as well as private plantation works (*ibid.*).

5.6   Research and Development

Initial scientific works were carried out by local people who conducted several crafts for production of their own materials and equipment for local use. They had their own Indigenous Knowledge (IK) of knowing the right raw materials, which included knowledge on minerals like iron ore bearing bed rocks. They smelt iron by using skilfully constructed iron smelting furnaces. After undertaking iron smelting through bloomery, they forged the iron into various implements like machetes, spears, hand hoes, knives and many others. Famous places for such iron works are spread all over the country including coastal areas, Katavi region, Rukwa region, Buhaya areas in Kagera region, Upare areas (with such technocrats called in Kipare as washana) and other areas.

Furthermore, many local people had knowledge on diseases and healing. They offered traditional medicine for various ailments. Early recruits were involved at various avenues, depending on *modus operandi* of a particular ethnic group (Saanane, 2004). Such training for skills in traditional medicine was and is still, useful in passing to the next generations, for the practices are still prevalent in Tanzanian societies.

Later on, early explorers and missionaries carried out scientific investigations in the country. They were from various disciplines that included geology, geography, palaeontology, agriculture and many others. Afterwards, during German rule, such endeavours were carried out. For instance, owing to garnet mineral prospects that were being carried out in Lindi, south-eastern Tanzania, in 1911, a Mining Engineer, B. Sattler got across dinosaur fossil bones at Tendaguru (Saanane and Magori, 1998; Zils *et al.*, 1995a, 1995b). Such discoveries led to recovery and a series of palaeontological expeditions that yielded a lot of dinosaur bones including complete skeletons designating for various dinosaur species (Saanane and Magori, 1998; Zils *et al.*, 1995a, 1995b). For instance, they recovered the following fossils: *Giraffatitan, brancai* (formerly known as *Brachiosaurus brancai*), *Brachisaurus africanus, Dicraeosaurus hansemani, Kentrurosaurus aethiopicus* and *Dsalotosaurus lettowvorbek* (Saanane and Magori, 1998; Zils *et al.*, 1995a, 1995b). Other types of organisms were recovered from Tendaguru locality that included the following: fish remains (described scientifcally as *Lepidotus minor*); over 150 bird remains depicting transition between birds and dinosaur evolution (*Rhamphorhynchus tendagurense*, and *Pterodactylus amingi*); in 1911, discovery of remains of the first mammals represented by a jaw (*Brancatherium tendagurense* later scientific analyses led to assignment of the remains to families belonging to either Paurodontidae or Peramuridae); invertebrate marine remains (represented by *Trigonia bomhardti, Belemnite rostrum, Aspidocerus richthofeni, Nautilus sp.* and *Perisphinctes sp.*); and fossil pollen remains represented by Classpollis (Zils *et al.*, 1995a, 1995b). Currently, there are few research endeavours in the vicinity owing to difficulties to carry out a full-swing research (see also, Zils et al., 1995a, 1995b).

Besides, in 1911, at Olduvai Gorge in Arusha region, northern Tanzania, the first discovery of human remains documenting human evolution was by a German Physician, Dr. Wilhelm Kattwinkel and in 1913, a German Geologist, Hanz Reck carried out scientific investigation in the area and code named the recovered specimens to Olduvai Hominid I [(OH 1) Matu *et al.*, 2017]. It is the first fossil to be discovered and the only *Homo sapiens*, recovered at the site (*ibid.*). The specimen was shipped to Germany and housed at Bavarian State Collection for Anthropology and Palaeoanatomy of Munich [(Germany) *ibid.*]. Moreover, German scientists discovered a lot of fossil humans and carried out a lot of research in palaeontology and geology, which facilitated later works, to date, for over a century with fascinating epochal discoveries that stirred the world beginning 1930s, 1950s as well as 1960s to date (see Magori, Saanane, and Schrenk, 1996).

In another vein, mining was facilitated by early expeditions by explorers and later others during German rule. They paved the way in gold mining at places like at Geita in Geita region and Senkenke in Singida region in 1909 (Bryceson *et al.*, 2012). Currently, there are many mining activities with huge investments in Geita region.

5.7 Discussion

It is important to re-iterate that this chapter is anchored on Afrocentricity Theory. It is pertinent for applying in the presented materials by safely arguing that the extant German built heritage in Tanzania is unquestionably important to the country's current use for socio-economic development. Such supposition is centred owing to the fact that the said built heritage does not denigrate Tanzania's stance on continued use and maintenance of such built heritage. It spans from tangible materials (infrastructure of many forms) to intangible heritage, notably the up-graded Kiswahili used from olden times including during German rule, to date, for official government use, national language and medium of instruction at elementary education level (primary school). Currently, Kiswahili language is used many fora (for example, since last year, 2023, the African Union permits its usage in its proceedings) and it has been accorded a commemorative day, the 7th July of every year by the United Nations.

In due regard, anchored on its outstanding premises, Afrocentricity Theory is significant for applying in the presented materials and thus, it is safe to argue the extant German built heritage in Tanzania is undeniably important to the country's current use for socio-economic development. It is centred on the fact that the said built heritage does not denigrate Tanzania's stance on continued use and maintenance of such built heritage. It spans from tangible materials (infrastructure of many forms) to intangible heritage, notably the up-graded Kiswahili used from olden times including during German rule, to date, for official government use, national language and medium of instruction at elementary education level (primary school). Therefore, the best position is that such heritage does not show discrimination by German authority and instead, it is a positive measure with many benefits to the country from olden times to date for socio-economic development.

It is clear that German rule established settlements in terms of buildings, infrastructure, cash crop cutlivation and actual social services for socio-economic development by then. Such heritage resources were crucial for later and current socio-economic development for independent Tanzania. The independent Tanzania benefits a lot from such ventures establihsed and developed by German rulers.

Set up of houses for residence and settlements at some urban areas by German authority were crucial start up and expansion of several clusters into towns. For instance, provision of Municipal status to early towns like Dar es Salaam and Tanga was a stepping stone for further development of buildings, infrastructure like roads and expansion of ports for cargo as well as passenger handling. The urban areas have grown as well as sprawled and thus, necessitated for according them city status later by the independent government. Some buildings, for instance, Old Boma at Mikindani in Mtwara was restored and conserved such that it nerves as a tourist hotel. The Old Boma in Arusha city houses the Arusha National Natural History Museum.

In another vein, initiation of agricultural undertakings for cash crops like cotton, sisal and the like for export were important by then and still are important for the country's socio-economic development. There are times in the late 1960s and 1970s, cash crops like sisal and cotton were leading export products as a result of such established agricultural undertakings. Additionally, between the late 1960s and 1970s, the country was able to establish textile industry in Dar es Salaam, Mwanza and later on, in Musoma. Thus, besides, export of raw cotton, the country exported finished processed cotton materials, clothes. Similarly, extensive sisal cultivation in the country facilitated establishment processing industries that were crucial big exports for the country. Currently, sisal production is given high impetus in its production in coastal areas of Tanga and immediate hinterland, specifically in areas of Morogoro region.

The country is still using and it has improved further infrastructure establishments, for example, the central railway from Dar es Salaam to Kigoma and the other Dar es Salaam, Tanga to Moshi line are still operative. They haul cargo and passengers all along the railway networks. Additionally, owing to such early development, particularly the central line (that was added between Tabora and Mwanza in absence of German rule), the government is in great progress constructing the Standard Gauge Railway (SGR) from Dar es Salaam to Kigoma and bifurcates at Tabora to Mwanza. The SGR will be extended from Uvinza in Kigoma region to Democratic Republic of Kongo via Burundi. All are fruits from German built central railway during its rule over a century ago.

The road network initiated by the German authority was a stepping stone for further development of roads in the country. The country has been and still is, building as well as maintaining roads by extending from already set up roads by German authority. Also, it up-graded many road networks in already set-up urban areas like Dar es Salaam, Tanga, Morogoro, Dodoma (now the country'capital), Tabora, Kigoma, Mwanza, Moshi, Arusha, Mtwara, Songea and many others.

Established social services during German rule such as schools and healthcare facilities are still beneficial to the country. For example, the set up Ocean Road Hospital is currently home for cancer patients, a specialised healthcare facility in the country. Under the new establishment, now Ocean Road Cancer Institute still collaborates with German like in 1990s, the entity carried out facelift of facilities with German development partner, Tanzania Tumor Aid Association Heidelberg e.V. Other health facilities, for example, Ndanda mission hospital in Mtwara region; Nyangao Mission hospital in Lindi region; Peramiho mission hospital in Ruvuma region; and several others have been developed into big health facilities catering for a big number of patients from many areas around the country.

Some ports that were in use for maritime trade were taken over by German rulers. They were given facelift, for example, Dar es Salaam port and Tanga port. These and other ports including the link with the railway line were and are still serving for import and export of commodities. Additionally, with the ship, M.V. Liemba still plying Lake Tanganyika waters (though intermittently stopping for maintainance) is a great assert for the country's socio-economic development. All such establishments and eventual developments have facilitated growth and sprawl of areas into big urban centres that have also increased their socio-economic ventures at various dimensions in the country.

Furthermore, establishment of dock yard and Customs Department by German rulers was extremely important later for the independent country's socio-economic development. It means that systematic cargo handling for import and export established by German authority paved the way for the independent country to continuosly give a facelift to such facilities around the country. Such areas that were linked with the railway, particularly end points like Kigoma in eastern Lake Tanganyika shores are important centres for import and export businesses together with link to neighbouring countries like the Democratic Republic of Congo and Burundi.

Moreover, set up of Customs Department meant systematic establishment of taxation system in the country by German authority for import and export of commodities. The country, as of mid-1990s, in its continued redress of the taxation system that includes revenue collection for import and export businesses, redressed ita revenue collection mandate by establishing the Tanzania Revenue Authority (TRA). All such measures are possible owing to the fact that for over a hundred years ago, the country has been with taxation system for local business ventures together with import and export of commodties.

Schools that were established under German rule acted as points of departure for further development in education. In fact, the early teachings at elementary level that also encompassed training in technical education are still beneficial to date. Moreover, such trainings involved use of medium of instruction, besides, Germany, Kiswahili. Importantly, German scholars were the first to develop Kiswahili language by publishing books such as the first Kiswahili dictionary, grammar and other language books. They made Kiswahili the official language and medium of instruction in the schools, both private (owned by missionaries) and government owned.

Kiswahili language is still the official medium of instruction in primary schools. Similar to unification of people by posting Kiswahili conversant officials around the country together with eventual spread of using Kiswahili, it united people such that it was used during non-violent independence struggles by local people. Of utmost importance, owing to such developments, the first president of independent Tanganyika (now mainland Tanzania), Mwalimu Julius Nyerere, in 1963, promulgated Kiswahili to be the national language. Moreover, there was the government circular in 1968 that requires use of Kiswahili language as the medium of instruction to all primary schools. Further developments in Kiswahili were spearhead by the then Prime Minister, in the early 1970s, Rashid Mfume Kawawa's order that Kiswahili language was the official and government language in all government communications, failing to which had to lead for no service offering to an individual not using Kiswahili in government business.

To date, Kiswahili is the medium of instruction in lementary schools. Moreover, there are degree courses in Kiswahili at universities such as University of Dar es Salaam and University of Dodoma. The former has Institute for Kiswahili Studies (Taasisi ya Taaluma za Kiswahili, TATAKI), while other universities have Kiswahili departments offering Kiswahili undergraduate and post-graduate degrees (master and doctoral degrees).

5.8 Future Prospects: Current Collaborations

5.8.1 General Overview

It is indisputable that built infrastructure by German authorities in Tanzania is still important to the current and future generations for socio-economic development. The existing built heritage in use must be properly maintained, conserved and preserved for sustainable use into future generations' socio-economic developments. Moreover, such built heritage documents and preserves the historic significance including potential of the country. It still offers many socio-economic benefits to the country.

Collaborative measures for facelift and social services with German authority as well as private entities are still important avenues to be considered and carried out sustainably. Moreover, all measures are possible due to the fact that the two countries (Tanzania and Germany) have long standing diplomatic ties. They have been and they are still collaborating for Tanzania's socio-economic development for many decades. Areas of operations range from health care, education, agriculture, economic cooperation and social matters. In fact, there is the German Cultural Centre, the Goethe Institute and thus, together with existing diplomatic relations that tells it all that bilateral cooperation is intact.

Moreover, German rule in Tanzania has many benefits. Currently, they are illuminated through several collaborative measures between Tanzania and the German Federal Government including developing partners in German. Much of the collaborations are beneficial not only to Tanzania but also to Germany.

References

Bangura, Abdul Karim (2012). "From Diop to Asante: Conceptualizing and Contextualizing the Afrocentric Paradigm." The Journal of Pan African Studies. 5(1): 103 – 125.

Baldus, R. D. (2001). "Wildlife Conservation in Tanganyika under German Colonial Rule." Internationale Afrikaforum 1(37): 73 – 78.

Bendix, Daniel (2012). "Colonial Power in Development: Tracing German Interventions in Population and Reproductive Health in Tanzania." PhD Thesis, Faculty of Humanities, University of Manchester.

Brenan, J.R. and Burton, A. (2007). "The emerging metropolis: A History of Dar es Salaam, circa 1862 – 2000," in Bernnan, J.R, Burton, A and Y. Lawi (Eds), *Dar es Salaam: Histories from an Emerging African Metropolis.* Nairobi: British Institute in Eastern Africa, pp. 13 – 75.

Bryceson, D. F., Jønsson, J. B., Kinabo, C. and Shand, M. (2012). "Unearthing treasure and trouble: mining as an impetus to urbanisation in Tanzania." Journal of Contemporary African Studies, 1-19. DOI: 10.1080/02589001.2012.724866

Edward, Frank and Hård, Mikael (2020). "Maintaining the local Empire: The Public Works Department in Dar es Salaam, 1920–60." The Journal of Transport History, 41(1): 27–46. DOI: 10.1177/0022526619883457.

Enns, Charis and Bersaglio, Brock (2020). "On the Coloniality of 'New' Mega-Infrastructure Projects in East Africa." Antipode 52(1): 101–123. doi: 10.1111/anti.12582.

Greiner, Andreas (2022). "Colonial Schemes and African Realities: Vernacular Infrastructure and the Limits of Road Building in German East Africa." The Journal of African History, 63(3), 328–347. Doi: 10.1017/S0021853722000500.

Khokholkova, Nadezhda (2016). "Afrocentricity: The Evolution of the Theory in the Context of American History." Social Evolution & History 15(1): 111–125.

Kirey, Reginald E. (2020). "A Long Way to Dodoma: Deconstructing Colonial Legacy by Relocating the Capital City in Tanzania." Tanzania Zamani, XII (1): 41-70.

Kironde, Lusugga (1994). "The Evolution of the Land use Structure of Dar es Salaam 1890-1990: A Study in the Effects of Land Policy," PhD Thesis, the University of Nairobi.

Larson, Lorne (2021). "Disease, Science and Religiosity: A Case of Leprosy in German East Africa." Tanzania Zamani, XIII (1): 1-43.

Lucian, Charles (2019). "Conservation, Maintenance and Repair of the Old Boma Historic Building in Bagamoyo, Tanzania." International Journal of Conservation Science. 10(3): 429-440.

Magai, Petro S. and Márquez-Velázquez, Alejandro (2011). "Tanzania's Mining Sector and Its Implications for the Country's Development." Berlin Working Papers on Money, Finance, Trade and Development, Working Paper No. 04/2011.

Magori, C. C., Saanane, C.B. & Schrenk, F. eds. (1996). Four Million Years of Hominid Evolution in Africa: Papers in Honour of Dr. Mary Douglas Leakey's Outstanding Contribution in Palaeoanthropology. KAUPIA. Darmstadter Beitrage Zur Naturgeschichte. Darmstadt. Heft 6:1 - 310.

Malik, Nasor (1996). "Extension of Kiswahili during the German Colonial Administration in continental Tanzania (former Tanganyika), 1885-1917." AAP, 47: 155-159

Matu, M., Crevecoeur, I. and Huchet, J.-B. (2017). "Taphonomy and Paleoichnology of Olduvai Hominid 1 (OH1), Tanzania." *International Journal of Osteoarchaeology*. DOI: 10.1002/oa.2593.

Mosha, Livin and Plevoets, Bie (2020). "Human Settlements and Architecture of Old Buildings in Historic Stone Towns: A Case of Bagamoyo Tanzania." International Research Journal of Engineering and Technology (IRJET). 7(04): 4936- 4947.

Saanane, Charles (2004). "Becoming a Traditional Healer: the Case of Wasukuma." Yusufu Lawi and Bertram Mapunda eds. History of Diseases and Healing in Africa. Proceedings of a Workshop held at the University of Dar es Salaam 20th December, 2003. GeGCA-NUFU Vol. 7: 72-79.

Saanane, C.B. & Magori, C.C. (1998). *Dinosaria wa* Tendaguru. Dar es Salaam: E & D Limited.

Shockley, K.G., & Frederick, R.M. (2010). "Constructs and dimensions of Afrocentric Education." Journal of Black Studies, *40*(6): 1212-1233.

United Republic of Tanzania [(URT) 2007]. *The Wildlife Conservation Policy*. Revised. Dar es Salaam: The Government Printer.

Watson, Marcia J. (2015). "Afrocentricity for All: A Case Study Examining the SelfHealing Power of Alternative Curricula as a Mediating Tool of Inclusion." PhD dissertation in Curriculum and Instruction, University of North Carolina at Charlotte.

Zils, W., Werner, C., Moritz, A. & Saanane, C. (1995a). "Tendaguru the Most Famous Locality of Africa. Review Survey and Future Prospects." DOCUMENTA NATURAE 97:1-41; MUNICH.

Zils, W., Werner, C., Moritz, A. & Saanane, C. (1995b). "Orientierende Tendaguru - Expedition 1994." Berliner geowiss. Abh., E 16.2: 483-531: Berlin.

CHAPTER SIX

RESPONSIBILITY IN GERMANY IN RELATION TO THE GENOCIDE OF MEMBERS OF THE MAJIMAJI MOVEMENT AND CIVIL SOCIETY IN 1905-1907 IN PRESENT-DAY TANZANIA

Prof. Dr. Claus Melter

6.1 Introduction

"At times, the German colonial empire covered around one million square kilometres and 12 million inhabitants. It was the third largest European colonial empire in terms of territory and the fifth largest in terms of population. (...) The present-day states of Namibia, Tanzania, Togo, Cameroon, Nigeria, Ghana, Rwanda, Burundi, Papua New Guinea, the Republic of the Marshall Islands, the Republic of Nauru, the Northern Mariana Islands, Palau, the Federated States of Micronesia and Western Samoa were wholly or partially under German colonial rule" (Dietrich/Strohschein 2011: 117).

The Germans also committed the first two genocides of the 20th century during the colonial era:

- the genocide of the Herero and Nama in Namibia between 1904 and 1908 with an estimated 80,000 to 100,000 deaths;
- the genocide of members of the Mahimaji movement and civil society from 1905 to 1907 in what is now Tanzania with up to 300,000 dead (see Genocide Alert 2012; Küppers-Adebisi A./Küppers-Adebisi M. 2023; von Riel 2023).

While the German colonial genocide committed against the Herero and Nama in present-day Namibia between 1904 and 1908 is now recognised as a fact by some academics and politicians after more than 30 years of engagement by descendants of the Herero and Nama who were attacked as well as civil society initiatives, a broad examination of the genocide in Tanzania is still pending. However, in addition to the many publications in Tanzania since the 1960s, there are now also some critical publications in German, such as those by Becker/Beez (2005); Bührer (2011); Bauche (2017); Haschemi Yekani (2019); and von Riel (2023). In the opposite in Tanzania, the German Genocide coommitted from 1905 to 1907 is presented in Books, Science and public Knowledge. Knowledge of German Genocide is part of the founding national narrative of Tanzania.

A little change can be seen in politics in Germany. In 2023, Federal President Steinmeier visited the Majimaj War Museum in Tanzania, spoke to descendants of persecuted and murdered groups and made a promise: "Germany is ready to come to terms with the past together. Nobody should forget what happened back then. And my great hope is that the joint reappraisal of the past will also involve young people in particular: Pupils, students, academics and museum professionals" (Federal President Steinmeier, 2023).

As in the above quote, politicians in power in Germany speak of accepting responsibility for past acts of violence during the colonial era and the commitment to coming to terms with the past, while at the same time avoiding clearly naming the genocide committed by Germans between 1905 and 1907 against the members of the Majimaji movement (cf. von Riel 2023). This ambivalence is also practised in order to avoid legal, moral and financial consequences resulting from the exact naming of the crimes (Bundeszentrale für politische Bildung 2021). In this sense, Savoy showed the European hypocracy speaking of Justice while not giving back the stolen african art objects since the demands from the 1960 to nowadays (Savoy 2021).

First, coming to terms with the colonial past in Germany faces the challenge that colonial violence is not fully recognised as a crime and genocide. Second, students, teachers and society have little knowledge about the German colonial era, in general and the colonial crimes in Tanzania, in particular. Third, there is a lack of interest in dealing with the colonial past (Terkessidis 2019; von Riel 2023). Fourth, there are a lot of activists, Non-Governmental Organizations (NGOs) and some scientists dealing with german colonial crimes. Fifth, politicians and dominant society prefer to continue racist colonial ideologie and exploitation (Palasie 2021) and do not want to take responsibility for colonial crimes, deported bodies and art objects (Savoy 20219:

Knowledge and discussions in Germany differ massively from the wealth of knowledge in Tanzania. In many cases, research on the genocide between 1905 and 1907 has not been recognised in Germany since the 1960s. There is no Resolution of the German Bundestag committing the Geman Genocide in Tanzania from 1905 to 1907.

While scholars in Tanzania have been talking about genocide in their analyses for decades (cf. Gwassa 1969; Gwassa 2005), the issue of genocide is rarely discussed in German- language publications (cf. Bührer 2011). In 2019, Bachmann and Kamp, in their detailed analysis of clarification of the question of genocide with regard to the proven intention, do not yet come to a clear statement in order to speak clearly of genocide in 2023 (Bachmann and Kemp 2019; Bachmann and Kemp 2023).

6.2 It was a genocide

According to the Convention on the Prevention and Punishment of the Crime of Genocide (UN Genocide Convention of 1948), the criteria for genocide are set out in Article 2 of the Convention

"In this Convention, genocide means any of the following acts,

which is committed with the intention of destroying a national, ethnic, racial or religious group as such in whole or in part:

a. Killing members of the group;
b. Causing serious physical or psychological harm to members of the group;
c. deliberately imposing living conditions on the group that are likely to cause its physical destruction in whole or in part;
d. Imposing measures aimed at preventing births within the group;
e. Forcibly transferring children of the group to another group" (https://www.voelkermordkonvention.de/uebereinkommen-ueber-die-verhuetung-und- bestrafung-des-voelkermordes-9217/).

Since both the intention to exterminate/destroy and criteria a, b, c and d can be proven in the German war against the Maji Maji, it is imperative to speak of genocide by German soldiers in Tanzania between 1905 and 1907 (cf. Baer/ Schroeter 2001; Becker/Beez 2005, Hall 2019; Bachmann and Kemp 2023; von Riel 2023).

In the specialist literature, the question of whether or not the individual criteria a to d of the UN Genocide Convention were fulfilled in the murders committed by Germans in Tanzania is consistently answered in the affirmative (see above). In the rarely detailed discussion as to whether the criterion of intent "to destroy, in whole or in part, a national, ethnical, racial or religious group as such" (UN Genocide Convention 1948) is met, there are various assessments (Bachmann/Kemp 2019; Bachmann Kemp 2023). Relevant here is the distinction made by the Federal Court of Justice in 2015, which distinguishes between instrumental genocide and genocide aimed at complete annihilation in the criterion of intent:

"An intention to commit genocide is also given if the intention of the perpetrator aims at the partial or complete destruction of the group in its social existence." (BGH 2015) 3. the destruction is also intended if it is a necessary means from the perpetrator's point of view to achieve a further underlying purpose. (Author's guidelines) StGB § 220a para. 1 old version BGH, judgement of. 21 May 2015 - 3 StR 575/14 (OLG Frankfurt a.M.)

Genocidal intent can, therefore, also be said to exist when part of an ethnic, religious, national or racialised group is to be partially destroyed in order to achieve, for example, the goal of subjugating or expelling the surviving group. In this sense, the intention to commit genocide can be clearly demonstrated on the basis of various quotations:

The governor responsible for Tanzania, Gustav Adolf Graf von Götzen, wrote in his 1909 volume "Deutsch-Ostafrika im Aufstand 1905/06" (von Götzen 1909) "in most cases, as this war has also proven, only such an approach will force the enemy to submit." Then one would arrive at a "milder view of this dira necessitas" (cruel necessity). Götzen knew what was at stake - he himself wrote of "extermination tactics." "When Götzen significantly increased the flat-rate "hut tax" for the locals in March 1905, resentment began to build. Now the charismatic Kinjikitile rallied the divided ethnic groups of the area behind him and called on them to revolt. On 29 July 1905, "the population began to riot," as a report to the governor put it, and one day later the German settler and cotton farmer Hans Hopfer died. An atrocity that was followed by hundreds of thousands of cruel deaths of natives" (Kellerhoff/Die Welt 02.11.2023, cf. also Hall 2020, p. 20ff.). And Captain Curt von Wangenheim, an officer in the German troops there, wrote "to Governor Gustav Adolf Graf von Götzen 'Only hunger and hardship can bring about a final subjugation. Military action alone will remain more or less a drop in the ocean. That was a commitment to genocidal action against the natives" (Kellerhoff/ Die Welt 02.11.2023).

With Oswald Masebo from the University of Dar es Salam (Mihanjo/ Masebo 2017; von Riel 2023), in view of the three-year period of killing and the up to 300,000 fighters and civilians killed by the Germans, one can, indeed must, undoubtedly speak of a systematically planned, ordered and practised genocidal intention (cf. Kemp/ Bachmann 2023). Surprisingly, the question and fact of the genocide carried out in Tanganyika, today's mainland Tanzania, is not addressed in many academic texts on the Majimaji War (cf. Bauche 2017; Kirey 2023).

6.3 Refusal to recognise the fact of crimes and genocides committed

On the one hand, the German Bundestag recognised the genocide of the Armenians by the Turks as a fact, as well as the Holodomor committed by the Russians in Ukraine and the genocide of the Yesid.

On the other hand, there were and still are no positively adopted resolutions recognising the fact of genocide in present-day Namibia and Tanzania in the German Bundestag. The Federal Government has always responded evasively to questions on this topic (cf. Federal Government 2023).

Addressing the genocide committed by Germans in Tanzania between 1905 and 1907 is the responsibility of politicians, especially in the Bundestag in Germany, who also have the task of working with civil society initiatives such as the Alliance Genocide does not expire or Berlin Postcolonial as well as descendants of the murdered groups, NGOs and academics in Tanzania to deal with the genocidal crimes committed by Germans in colonial Tanzania.

6.4 The power of dethematisation

It is the height of power to commit a genocide before the eyes of the world, not to be punished for it and to bring it into almost complete oblivion. Politicians and academics in Germany "succeeded" in concealing the genocides committed against the Herero and Nama between 1904 and 1908 (cf. Zimmerer/Zeller 2003) until the 2000s, when the genocide was increasingly addressed politically and academically due to the decades-long commitment of the Herero and Nama in Namibia, academics and civil society groups in Namibia and Germany, and then taken up and negotiated by the governments of both countries. However, this took place without the elected representatives of the Herero and Nama, who disagreed to the proposed agreements and have been systematically demanding for their participation, apology, repatriation of skulls, bodies and cultural artefacts as well as reparations for decades to this day. Many of the actors clarify their positions in the book *Generation Repair: Transnational Dialogues Namibia – Germany* (Küppers-Adebisi A./Küppers-Adebisi M. 2023), edited by Adetoun Küppers- Adebisi/ Michael Küppers-Adebisi 2023.

As far as Tanzania and the genocide committed there are concerned, Germany has yet to engage in a broad academic and political debate on the genocide committed there. Federal President Steinmeier's visit to the Majimaji War Memorial Museum and talks with the descendants of murdered groups in 2023 may be an important point of change, but the Federal Government and the Federal President have not yet followed up their declarations of intent with action, as the Federal Government's answer to a question from MP Gesine Lötzsch shows. To the question: "In the view of the Federal Government, was the killing of up to 300,000 people (1905 to 1907) in what is now Tanzania a genocide, and if not, why not? Answer given by State Secretary Dr Thomas Bagger on 24 January 2024/Federal Government): (Schriftliche Fragen mit den in der Woche vom 22. Januar 2024 eingegangenen Antworten der Bundesregierung - translated: Only general statements were made to the effect that the governments were in discussion with each other (Bundestag printed matter 20/10170 (bundestag.de) https://dserver.bundestag.de/btd/20/101/2010170.pdf).

The genocide of the supporters of the Maji Maji movement and civil society in Tanzania between 1905 and 1907 is also trivialised and concealed by the Federal Agency for Civic Education (http://www.bpb.de/politik/hintergrund-aktuell/209829/1905-der-maji-maji- aufstand) using obfuscating terms such as "uprising." An "uprising" appears as an unlawful action against a legal government. Le Gall and Mboro (2019) refer to the Majimaji War, which was waged by the Germans. There is the Majimaji War Museum in Tanzania (MajiMaji War Museum, Songea, Tanzania - Imagining Futures https://imaginingfutures.world/people/majimaji-war-museum-songea-tanzania/) and many critical and reflective academic texts talk about a war at that time (Mihanjo/ Masebo 2017; Le Gall/ Mboro 2019; von Riel 2023).

The question of whether or not genocide was carried out by the Germans in Tanzania is also being debated in the German Federal Foreign Ministry. Following the request by Katja Keul, Minister of State at the Federal Foreign Office, in 2023 to reappraise Tanzanian-German colonial history (Deutschlandfunk 20 March 2023), four working groups on German colonial history in Tanzania were set up, according to oral information provided to the author by the Federal Foreign Ministry:

1. Issues relating to the return of human remains of Tanzanian people held by German museums and other institutions in Germany.
2. Issues relating to the restitution of cultural artefacts stolen from Tanzania during the colonial era that are held by German museums and other institutions in Germany.
3. Scientific cooperation between Tanzanian and German universities and scientists (according to an email from the participating Professor Dr. Brockmeyer, the content of the 2024 project will focus exclusively on medical history research)
4. Questions of scientific terminology about the events in Tanzania from 1884 to 1918.

As outlined above, the latter working group must come to the conclusion that the Germans committed genocide. The latter group has not yet published any statement. Nor did the Federal President use the word crime or genocide in Tanzania.

6.5 Remembering the victims of National Socialism

Mentioning the names of those persecuted and murdered during the National Socialist era is an act of honouring their lives, their personalities, their biographies and their suffering. The Jewish victims of the Holocaust in particular are rightly commemorated. In recent decades, other groups of victims have also been increasingly commemorated. The book "Das Vergessen der Vernichtung, ist Teil der Vernichtung selbst" (Fuchs/Rotzoll *et al.*, 2007) presents 23 biographies of people who were killed as part of the murder of the sick (cynically called "euthanasia" = beautiful death). As in the texts by Gudrun Silberzahn-Jandt (2015), there is the opportunity to get to know the individuality and wishes of the people, to identify with them and to develop empathy. On 27 January 2020, the 75th anniversary of the liberation of the Auschwitz concentration camp, learning from the history of violence is rightly called for. A first step is undoubtedly to familiarise ourselves with the acts carried out and the people involved. In Yad Vasehm it says: "To learn from history, you have to learn history." Loosely translated, this means that in order to learn from history, history must first be learnt, known and dealt with.

6.6 Different memory practices

However, there are significant differences in the practices of remembering the victims of colonialism and National Socialism in Germany. In contrast to these important practices is the concealment of genocides such as those committed against the Herero and Nama in 1904-1908 in present-day Namibia and the genocide in the Majimaji War of 1905-1907, both perpetrated by Germans. In Germany, no government has recognised the genocides in Namibia and Tanzania as culpable genocides. Especially since the Armenia resolution of the Bundestag, where Turkey was called upon to commemorate and confess the genocide carried out between 1914 and 1917, it is more than morally reprehensible that the German government does not recognise the fact that genocides were carried out. On the one hand, the federal governments want to avoid paying compensation and reparations and, on the other, they do not want to discuss the continuity of racist thought, action and extermination practices from colonialism to National Socialism in Germany. In schools and universities, the majority of pupils and students are taught very little about German colonialism and the colonial genocides. The dominant historical scholarship also plays a significant role in concealing the violence of colonialism.

The so-called primal catastrophe of the 20th century was not the First World War, but the genocides committed in the context of colonialism. For it was here that the construction of human groups, their hierarchisation, legal and social inequality and the extermination of human groups were systematically practised for the first time. Hundreds of thousands of people were murdered to realise their own economic and military interests. A pattern that was then also applied in the Holocaust, a breach of civilisation (Zimmerer 2011).

6.7 Concealment of genocides in writings on missions and colonial medicine

Even authors with racism-critical ambitions remain silent about the genocide when talking about the colonial period in Tanzania (see Brahm/Brockmeyer 2014). The majority of academic works on Tanzania, including those on the period from 1900 to 1945, do not address the Majimaji War. This disregards both the relevance of the genocide to the issues addressed and the ethical and political demands of commemorating the persecuted and murdered.

In 2017, Helen-Kathrin Treutler wrote in her book "Christliches Missionsverständnis und nationalsozialistische Weltanschauung". The Bethel Mission between 1933-1945" about the influence of National Socialist ideas on the Bethel Mission in Tanzania during the National Socialist era. The genocide committed by Germans in Tanzania is not mentioned with a single line or footnote, not even in the history of Tanzania from 1884 to 1945. What was the presence of German missionaries in Tanzania like for the colonised people living there, who will all have known about the genocide? What influence did this have on the utilisation of missionary or medical services (for example, the "lunatic asylum" in Luitundi, run by the Bethel Mission; for a critical perspective: Hamilton 2009)? How did the military, police, mission and medicine work together (cf. Hamilton 2009)? What was the significance of co-operation with the violent colonial government? The failure to address the genocide systematically leaves important questions about the relationship between colonial rule and the Bethel Mission and its African addressees unanswered.

Manuela Bauche writes about the central findings of her highly readable study on "Medizin und Herrschaft. Malaria control in Cameroon, East Africa and East Frisia 1890-1919 (Bauche 2017), about the violent enforcement of colonial rule, whereby colonial medicine helped to establish rule and profited from the colonial rule in whose protection it worked. While in Germany it was primarily poorer, working "white" people who were affected, in the colonies both the legal separation into Europeans and Africans (into "natives" and "non-natives", cf. Bauche 2017, p. 15) and the racist attributions in relation to (un)civilisedness and the risk of infection were fundamental (cf. Bauche 2017; 357ff.). Nationality was often conceptualised in the context of racist constructions (cf. also El-Tayeb 2001). In order to establish domination and colonial medicine, contacts were established with regional contact persons who were supposed to mediate the interests of the rulers and the physicians, reduce/break resistance and enforce the interests of domination and research on the ground. In contrast to the fight against malaria in East Frisia, coercion and violence were used in Cameroon and today's Tanzania in Africa to carry out quite dangerous medical experiments on patients (see also Bauche 2006; Eckart 1997). However, the German soldiers who committed the genocide were also part of the fight against malaria and were treated as a precaution or for existing malaria diseases. The Lebendiges Museum Online of the Deutsches Historisches Museum assumes that around 180,000 Tanzanians were killed by starvation or rifle bullets (LEMO 2017: https://www.dhm.de/lemo/kapitel/kaiserreich/aussenpolitik/maji-maji-krieg.html).

The historian Gwassa from the Majimaji Research Project estimates that 250,000 to 300,000 people were killed (cf. Gwassa 1969; Baer/Schröter 2001). A third of the population in the war zone died (cf. LEMO 2017). The survivors' health was severely weakened by the practice and policy of scorched earth, specifically by the burning of entire villages, fields and homes, the killing of animals and the capture of women and children, while the men were shot (cf. Baer/ Schröter 2001; Becker/ Beez 2005; Hall 2019).

6.8   Colonial medicine and genocide

As a rule, sick Tanzanians could only go to the "native" hospitals, as the European doctors mainly or exclusively cared for European/German patients and the military doctors for soldiers. The medical reports show that malaria was one of the main illnesses among the latter (cf. Morlong 2002). The overall health of the population was thus significantly influenced both by the Majimaji War and by the violent punitive expeditions following the 76 military resistance actions by Tanzanians (cf. Bundeszentrale für politische Bildung 2017), and malaria diseases played an important role among both the colonised and the whites, including the soldiers. What is successful in Manuela Bauche's study, however, is that she addresses both the violence of the harmful medical experiments (cf. Bauche 2006) and the continuities of colonial doctors who were also involved in Nazi medicine in legislation and research (cf. Bauche 2017).

6.9   Learning history

Interested parties, researchers, teachers and students who deal with colonialism, genocides and violence and the question of what can be learnt from history should read as well as consider the reports of the survivors of violence and genocides in Tanzania alongside the reports of the colonisers (cf. Gwassa 1969; Hussein 1969; Baer/ Schröter 2001; Becker/Beez 2005; Laurien 2005; Saavedra Casco 2005). In addition, the question of the relationship between colonialism and National Socialism as well as today's social relations influenced by racism appears more urgent than ever. The economic, legal and social profiteers of the German genocide, such as the German state, farmers and missionaries, must acknowledge their shared responsibility and guilt, apologise, pay reparations and tackle land reforms, and return the skulls including bones of the murdered Tanzanians, as well as stolen cult and ritual objects.

Dealing with colonial medicine is also important for medical-historical research into the murder of the sick: What is the relationship between medical experiments and these periods? Which people, like Eugen Fischer, were colonial physicians and then researchers and participants in legislative procedures under National Socialism (see interview with Manuela Bauche Taz 6 May 2019)? How did "eugenic" and racist logics of dehumanisation, rationalisation and objectification of people develop in politics, the military, religion, medicine and society? What analytical and moral insights can be gained from the examination of colonial and Nazi medicine for today's medical and social professions and research?

It will be crucial to finally take note of the texts and research from Tanzania in Germany in order to find ways to come to terms with the colonial crimes committed by Germans in cooperation with researchers, NGOs and politicians from Tanzania and to take responsibility in the sense of clarification, recognition of the fact of genocide, repatriation and reparations.

Sources and literature

Akakpo-Numado, Sena Yawo (2005): Mädchen- und Frauenbildung in den deutschen Afrika-Kolonien (1884-1914) Inaugural-Dissertation. Universität Bochum.

Bachmann/ Kempf (2023): 300,000 Tanzanians were killed by Germany during the Maji-Maji uprising – it was genocide and should be called that (theconversation.com), https://theconversation.com/300-000-tanzanians-were-killed-by-germany-during-the-maji-maji-uprising-it-was-genocide-and-should-be-called-that-217712 (Recherchedatum 15.07.2024)

Bachmann, Klaus/ Kemp, Gerhard (2021): Was Quashing the Maji-Maji Uprising Genocide? An Evaluation of Germany's Conduct through the Lens of International Criminal Law. Holocaust and Genocide Studies, Volume 35, Issue 2, Fall 2021, Pages 235–249, https://doi.org/10.1093/hgs/dcab032 (Recherchedatum 15.07.2024)

Bagger, Thomas/ Bundesregierung (24. Januar 2024): Antwort der Bundesregierung auf die Frage der fraktionslosen Abgeordneten Dr.

Gesine Lötzsch: War aus Sicht der Bundesregierung die Tötung von bis zu 300.000 Personen (1905 bis 1907) im heutigen Tansania ein Genozid, und wenn nein, warum nicht? Drucksache 20/10170 (bundestag.de) https://dserver.bundestag.de/btd/20/101/2010170.pdf (Recherchedatum 20.07.2024)

Baer, Martin/ Schröter, Olaf (2001): Eine Kopfjagd. Deutsche in Ostafrika. Berlin: Ch. Links Verlag

Bauche, Manuela (2019): "Kolonialismus ist auch eine Geschichte der Verdrängung". https://taz.de/Euthanasie/!5589559/ (Berlin Interview geführt von Hannah El-Hitami 6.5.2019; Recherchedatum 20.02.2020)

Bauche, Manuela (2017): Medizin und Herrschaft. Malariabekämpfung in Kamerun, Ostafrika und Ostfriesland (1890-1919). Frankfurt/ New York: Campus

Bauche Manuela (2006) Robert Koch, die Schlafkrankheit und Menschenexperimente im kolonialen Ostafrika. Freiburg. Zu finden unter: http://www.freiburg-postkolonial.de/Seiten/robertkoch.html (Recherchedatum 22.01.2020)

Becker, Felicitas/ Beez, Jigal (Hrsg.) (2005): Der Maji-Maji-Krieg in Deutsch-Ostafrika 1905-1907. Berlin: Ch. Links Verlag

Bührer, Tanja (2011): Die kaiserliche Schutztruppe für Deutsch-Ost-Afrika. Koloniale Sicherheitspolitik und transkulturelle Kriegsführung 1885-1918. München: De Gruyther Oldenbourg-Verlag.

Bundespräsident Steinmeier, Frank Walter (2023): Rede Besuch des Majimaji-Museums in Songea, November 2023; Der Bundespräsident - Reden und Interviews - Besuch des Maji-Maji-Museums (bundespraesident.de) https://www.bundespraesident.de/SharedDocs/Reden/DE/Frank-Walter-Steinmeier/Reden/2023/11/231101-Songea-Maji-Maji-Museum.html (Recherchedatum 17.07.2024)

Bundesregierung (2023): Antwort der Bundesregierung auf die Kleine Anfrage der Abgeordneten Sevim Dağdelen, Cornelia Möhring, Andrej Hunko, weiterer Abgeordneter und der Fraktion DIE LINKE.– Drucksache 20/6551 –Die Bundesregierung und die Aufarbeitung der Kolonialverbrechen auf dem Gebiet des heutigen Tansanias. Drucksache 20/6943, 24.05.2023 (Recherchedatum 17.07.2024)

Bundeszentrale für politische Bildung (2015): 1905: Der Maji Maji-Aufstand gegen die deutsche Kolonialherrschaft. Bonn: http://www.bpb.de/

politik/hintergrund-aktuell/209829/1905-der-maji-maji-aufstand (Recherchedatum 10.12.2019)

Bundeszentrale für politische Bildung (2020): Vor 115 Jahren: Der Maji-Maji-Aufstand. Bonn https://www.bpb.de/kurz-knapp/hintergrund-aktuell/209829/vor-115-jahren-der-maji-maji-aufstand/ (Recherchedatum 17.07.2024)

Brahm, Felix/ Brockmeyer, Bettina (Hrsg.) (2014): Koloniale Spurensuche in Bielefeld und Umgebung. Bielefeld: tpk-Verlag.

Brüntjen, Jana-Sophie (2020): Eine weiße Geschichte. Wie die deutsche Kolonialgeschichte an Schulen gelehrt wird. Migazin Online-Magazin. Düsseldorf. 23.09.2020. Weiß: Wie die deutsche Kolonialgeschichte an Schulen unterrichtet wird (migazin.de) (Recherchedatum 17.07.2024)

Deutschlandfunk (20.03.2023): Auswärtiges Amt. Deutschland will Kolonialgeschichte in Tansania aufarbeiten Auswärtiges Amt - Deutschland will Kolonialgeschichte in Tansania aufarbeiten (deutschlandfunk.de) https://www.deutschlandfunk.de/deutschland-will-kolonialgeschichte-in-tansania-aufarbeiten-100.html (Recherchedatum 21.07.2024)

Dietrich, Anette/Strohschein, Juliane (2011): Deutscher Kolonialismus. In Arndt, Susan/Ofuatey-Alazard, Nadja (Hrsg.): Wie Rassismus aus Wörtern spricht. (K)Erben des Kolonialismus im Wissensarchiv deutsche Sprache. Ein kritisches Nachschlagewerk. Münster: Unrast-Verlag, S. 114-120.

Eckart, Wolfgang U. (1997): Medizin und Kolonialimperialismus 1884-1945. Paderborn u.a.: Schöningh.

El-Tayeb, Fatima (2001): Schwarze Deutsche. Der Diskurs um "Rasse" und nationale Identität 1890-1933. Frankfurt am Main.

Fuchs, Petra u.a. (Hrsg.) (2007) »Das Vergessen der Vernichtung ist Teil der Vernichtung selbst« Lebensgeschichten von Opfern der nationalsozialistischen »Euthanasie«. Göttingen: Wallstein.

Graf von Götzen, Gustav Adolf (1909): "Deutsch-Ostafrika im Aufstand 1905/06": ((von Götzen 1909)

Genocide Alert (2012): Der Völkermord an den Herero und Nama (1904-1908). https://www.genocide-alert.de/projekte/deutschland-und-massenverbrechen/herero-und-nama/ (Recherchedatum 22.07.2024)

Gwassa, Gilbert Clement Kamana (1969): The German intervention and African resistance in Tanzania. In: Kimambo, Isaria N./ Temu, A. J. (Hg.): A history of Tanzania. Nairobi, S.85-122.

Gwassa, Gilbert Clement Kamana (2005): The Outbreak and Development oft he Majimaji-War 1905 – 1907. Köln.G

Gwassa, Gilbert C. K. & Iliffe John (Hrsg.) (1968): Record of the Maji Maji Rising. Part One, Nairobi.

Hall, Lucy (2019): Deutscher Kolonialismus in Tansania. In: Ausstellung Soziale Arbeit, Medizin und Nationalsozialismus. Fachhochschule Bielefeld.

Hamilton Majida (2009): Mission im kolonialen Umfeld. Deutsche protestantische Missionsgesellschaften in Deutsch-Ostafrika. Göttingen: Universitäts-Verlag Göttingen.

Haschemi Yekani, Minu (2019): Koloniale Arbeit, Rassismus, Migration und Herrschaft in Tansania (1885-1914). Frankfurt a.M/ New York: Campus

Hussein Ebrahim (1969) KINJEKETILE Nairobi: Oxford University Press Nacherzählt von Lourenco Noronha Lektor (1974-2009) für Swahili-Literatur am Institut für Afrikawissenschaften der Universität Wien Taasisi ya Taaluma ya Bara la Afrika Chuo Kikuu cha Vienna Stand: Mai 2009.

Ebner, Elzear. 1987. The History of the Wangoni and Their Origin in the South African Bantu Tribes. Peramiho: Benedictine Publications.

Gulliver, P.H. 1955. "A History of the Songea Ngoni." Tanganyika Notes and Records 41, 16–30.

Iliffe, John (1979): A Modern History of Tanganyika. Cambridge

Illiffe, John (1969):Tanganyika under German Rule, 1905–1912, Cambridge

Kellerhoff, Sven Felix (2023): Die planmäßge Schädigung der Bevölkerung ist unerläßlich! Artikel Die Welt Steinmeier in Tansania: Völkermord in Deutsch-Ostafrika 1905/06 - WELT (Recherchedatum 17.07.2024)

Kirey, Reginald Elias (2023): Memories of German Colonialism in Tanzania. Berlin/ Boston de Gruyter

Künkler, Eva (2022): Koloniale Gewalt in Deutsch-Neuguinea und der Raub kultureller Objekte und menschlicher Überreste. Eine systematische

Übersicht zu Militärgewalt und sogenannten Strafexpeditionen in deutschen Kolonialgebieten in Ozeanien (1884–1914). Magdeburg: Deutsches Zentrum Kulturgutverluste Kuenkler.9783593506234.pdf (Recherchedatum 17.07.2024)

Küppers-Adebisi, Adetoun / Küppers-Adebisi Michael (Hrsg.) (2023): Generation Repair: Transnationale Dialoge Namibia – Deutschland. Berlin: AfrotakTV cybernomads.

Kuß, Susanne (2010): Deutsches Militär auf kolonialen Kriegsschauplätzen. Eskalation von Gewalt zu Beginn des 20. Jahrhunderts (Studien zur Kolonialgeschichte, Bd. 3., Berlin: Ch. Links Verlag.

Laurien, Ingrid (2005): "Zu keiner Zeit konnten wir sagen: Jetzt haben wir Frieden." Berichte afrikanischer Zeitzeugen. In: Becker, Felicitas/ Beez, Jigal (Hg.): Der Maji-Maji-Krieg in Deutsch-Ostafrika. 1905-1907. Berlin, S.115-121.

Lebendiges Museum Online (2017): Der Maji Maji Krieg. Berlin. Zu finden unter: https://www.dhm.de/lemo/kapitel/kaiserreich/aussenpolitik/maji-maji-krieg.html (Recherchedatum 22.01.2020)

Le Gall, Yann/ Mboro, Mnyaka Sururu (2019): Remembering the Dismembered. African Human Remains and Memory Cultures in and after Repatriation. A thesis submitted in fulfillment of the requirements for the degree of Doctor of Philosophy Remembering_the_Dismembered_African_Huma.pdf (Recherchedatum 17.07.2024)

Masebo, Oswald (2016): Video: Dr. Oswald Masebo (University of Dar es Salam): Postcolonial Memory: A Shared Legacy: Tanzania-Germany" Video: Dr. Oswald Masebo (University of Dar es Salam) „Postcolonial Memory: A Shared Legacy: Tanzania-Germany" – Hamburgs (post-) koloniales Erbe (uni-hamburg.de)

Mihanjo, Eginald P.A.N./ Masebo, Oswald (2017): Maji Maji War, Ngoni Warlords and Militarism in Southern Tanzania A Revisionist View of Nationalist History. journal of african military history 1 (2017) 41-71

Melter, Claus (2018): Migration, Gender und Bildung – und Klasse, Behinderung etc.? Historische und herrschaftskritische Überlegungen. In: Wegner, Anke/ Dirim, Inci (Hrsg.): Normative Grundlagen und reflexive Verortungen im Feld DaF_DaZ*. Verlag Barbara Budrich, S. 23-44

Melter, Claus (2020): Das Verschweigen von kolonialen Völkermorden setzt die Logik der Vernichtung fort – Claus Melter | politeknik.de

Morlong, Thomas (2002): "Ich habe die Sache satt hier, herzlich satt." Briefe des Kolonialoffiziers Rudolf von Hirsch aus Deutsch-Ostafrika 1905-1907. http://www.freiburg-postkolonial.de/Seiten/BriefeKolonialoffizierHirsch.pdf (Recherchedatum 22.01.2020)

Ogunniyi Ekemode, Gabriel (1973): GERMAN RULE IN NORTH-EAST TANZANIA, 1885 – 1914. University of London. School of Oriental and African Studies University of London, London.

Palasie, Serge (2021): Rassismus – Zur überwindung eines kolonialideolgischen Auslaufmodells. In: Zeller, Joachim Bechhaus-Gerst, Marianne (Hrsg.) (2021): Deutschland postkolonial? Die Gegenwart der imperialen Vergangenheit. , aktualisierte und erweiterte Auflage. Berlin: Metropol-Verlag, S. 505-524.

Saavedra Casco, José Arturo (2005): Die Suche nach dem Mittelweg. Das Maji-Maji-Gedicht des Swahili-Dichters Abdul Karim Jamaliddini. In: Becker, Felicitas/ Beez, Jigal (Hg.): Der Maji-Maji-Krieg in Deutsch-Ostafrika. 1905-1907. Berlin, S.133-142.

Savoy, Bénédicte (2021): Afrikas Kampf um seine Kunst. Geschichte einer postkolonialen Niederlage. München: C.H. Beck-Verlag.

Silberzahn-Jandt, Gudrun (2015): Esslingen am Neckar im System von Zwangssterilisation und "Euthanasie" während des Nationalsozialismus. Ostfildern: Thorbecke.

Spieker, Susanne (2015): Die Entstehung der modernen Erziehungswissenschaft in der europäischen Expansion. Frankfurt am Main u.a.: Peter Lang

Tanzania Network (2023): Forderungskatalog anlässlich der Reise von Bundespräsident Frank-Walter Steinmeier nach Songea (Tansania) am 01.11.2023 Unsere Forderungen | Tanzania-Network.de (Recherchedatum 17.07.2024)

Terkessidis, Mark (2021): Das postkoloniale Klassenzimmer. Berlin: Aktion Courage. Baustein_12-WEB.pdf (schule-ohne-rassismus.org) Recherchedatum 17.07.2024)

Terkessidis, Mark (2019): Wessen Erinnerung zählt? Koloniale Vergangenheit und Rassismus heute. Hamburg. Hoffmann und Campe.

Treutler, Helen-Kathrin (2017): Christliches Missionsverständnis und nationalsozialistische Weltanschauuung. Die Bethelmission zwischen 1933-1945. Bielefeld: Luther-Verlag

UN 1948: https://www.voelkermordkonvention.de/uebereinkommen-ueber-die-verhuetung-und-bestrafung-des-voelkermordes-9217/ (Recherchedatum 22.01.2020).

von Riel, Aert (2023): Der verschwiegene Völkermord. Deutsche Kolonialverbrechen in Ostafrika. Köln: Papyrossa-Verlag.

Zeller, Joachim Bechhaus-Gerst, Marianne (Hrsg.) (2021): Deutschland postkolonial? Die Gegenwart der imperialen Vergangenheit., aktualisierte und erweiterte Auflage. Berlin: Metropol-Verlag.

Zimmerer, Jürgen/ Zeller, Joachim (2003): Völkermord in Deutsch-Südwestafrika Untertitel: Der Kolonialkrieg (1904-1908) in Namibia und seine Folgen Berlin: Ch. Links-Verlag.

THE EDITORS AND AUTHORS

Dr. Sakina Faru is lecturer at Saint Augustine University of Tanzania (SAUT). She was a Post-Doctoral fellow at Vechta University (October, 2021 – April, 2022); and from April to September, 2022 she was visiting fellow at Hochschule Bielefeld, University of Applied Sciences and Arts, Germany. She teaches undergraduate and post-graduate students in Journalism and Mass Communication. Areas of specialisation and interest include Journalism and Mass Communication; Gender and Diversity; and Cultural Anthropology. Extra mural duties include Matron of Peer Educators at SAUT and member of Gender Desk at SAUT.

Prof. Dr. Claus Melter, teaches at Bielefeld University. His focus is on human rights-oriented and anti-discrimination and anti-racism-ambitious social work in a migrant society. He also researches colonialism and National Socialism, especially infant muder in WW II. He works for Decided against Racism and Discrimination e. V. and the Bielefeld University Bethel Research Group on National Socialism. Latest Publication: Degen, Barbara/ Keßler, Marion/ Melter, Claus (2024.): Ermordet in Bethel? Neue Forschungen zu Säuglingssterblichkeit und Hirnforschung in der NS-Zeit. Verlagsgruppe Beltz, Juventa: Weinheim/ Basel. Melter, Claus (Ed.) (2021): Diskriminierungs- und rassismuskritische Soziale Arbeit und Bildung. Weinheim/Basel: Beltz.

Dr. Charles Saanane is a retiree from University of Dar es Salaam, Department of Archaeology and Heritage Studies. Currently, he is an adjunct fellow at University of Dodoma, Department of Archaeology and History. His main teaching and research interests along with areas of specialization include Palaeontology (encompassing human evolution, dinosaur research and Forensic Anthropology), Ethnoarchaeology and History. He is founding and Executive Committee member of Eastern African Association for Palaeoanthropologists and Palaeontologists (EAAPP). His research collaborations with international scientists involved him at various places including world famous palaeoanthropological sites - Olduvai Gorge, Laetoli and Makuyuni.